High Adventure in Dangerous
and Heavenly Places

MISSION PILOT

The David Gates Story

EILEEN E. LANTRY

D1417675

Pacific Press® Publishing Association
Nampa, Idaho
Oshawa, Ontario, Canada
www.pacificpress.com

Edited by Tim Lale
Cover design by Tim Larson
Inside design by Steve Lanto
Cover and inside photos © by Ted Burgdorff

Additional copies of this book may be purchased at
http://www.adventistbookcenter.com

Library of Congress Cataloging-in-Publication Data:

Lantry, Eileen E.
 Mission pilot : high adventure in dangerous places : the David Gates
story / Eileen E. Lantry.
  p. cm.
 ISBN: 0-8163-1870-0
  1. Gates, David Lee, 1959-2. Missionaries—Latin America—Biography. 3. Bush pilots—Latin America—Biography. 4. Seventh-day
Adventists—Latin America—Biography. 5.Missionaries—United
States—Biography. I. Title.

 BV2832.2.G38 L36 2002
 266'.67'092—dc21
 [B]   2001051371

02 03 04 05 06 • 5 4 3 2 1

CONTENTS

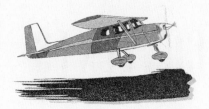

Foreword

We believe in God, we know He exists, we see His handiwork, and we say we trust Him unconditionally. Then why are we surprised when He works marvels in our lives?

Mission Pilot shouts to the world God's great deeds and His direct, remarkable intervention in the lives of David and Becky Gates.

You'll recognize God's miraculous hand in manipulating infant David's internal organs so they'll function. You'll see why God impressed eight-year-old David to ask a special girl to marry him when he gets big. You'll understand why God saved teenage David in a plane crash, and shudder when David feels a gun in his back as his plane is hijacked. You'll have no doubt that God chose David and Becky for specialized service when He called, prepared, led, and guided them to take their five children to a jungle village with no financial backing, depending totally on God.

For those of us who have admired David through the years, this book confirms our appreciation. The beautiful part is that the end of the story cannot be told, because it has not yet been lived. As I write this, David, his beloved Rebecca, and their children still serve in the jungles of South America. Almost daily God opens new vistas with direct signs and intervention for his mission work to expand. Many stories will follow to increase your love for God and your admiration of a missionary couple who gladly choose this way of life to honor God and serve Him in dangerous places.

At this time, when material things engross the world, I find it refreshing to know and see how the Lord still calls, equips, and sends missionaries to depend wholly on Him in their service. Your life will be blessed and enriched by the dedicated service of the Gates family. So, in your mind and spirit, join them in the simple jungle life, fly over vast stretches of rain forest, experience angel protection when robbers in the cities assaulted them, knowing God will keep you too.

As you pray for David, his family, and the Amerindians of South America, count your blessings. Then ask yourself, "Do I practice the contented life of constant trust in God's leading in the work God has called me to do?"

Israel Leito, President
Inter-American Division of Seventh-day Adventists
Miami, Florida
September 2001

A most recent family picture taken at
Katrina's graduation from Laurelbrook Academy (2001).
Back row, L to R: Katia, Carlos, Lina.
Front row, L to R: Becky, Katrina, David, Kristopher.

In the airplane (Cessna 185) about to begin flight to Mexico.

Hijacked!

"Doesn't look good, professor. Fog has socked in the Highlands."

David Gates, an American mission pilot in his mid-twenties, leaned forward in the cockpit of the Cessna 185 Skywagon and scanned the horizon. Thick clouds were draped low over the Sierra Madre of southern Mexico.

"Must have rained heavily all day around here," he continued. "I'm afraid the little airstrip by our hospital will be totally unsafe for landing." He spoke clear, precise Spanish with a Bolivian accent to the older Mexican man sitting in the copilot seat.

"What's the problem, *Capitán?*"

"The airstrip is in a low place. If the short grass is covered with water, the surface becomes as slick as ice. Even at a slow landing speed, the brakes become useless. I'd have no control over the plane, and we would crash into a tree." With more than ten years of experience as a pilot, David knew the danger they faced. He sat tense and stiff.

"So what shall we do?" Professor Chente asked.

"I'll fly low and circle the area several times. Maybe we can find a flat place on higher ground." The plane began to lose altitude and dropped below the clouds.

"There it is." He pointed to the left. The rays of the setting sun highlighted the compound of the mission hospital, high school, and nursing school. Clustered around the perimeter were the homes of the doctor, nurses, and other workers. "See that little house near the landing strip—that's where my family lives. I'm sure Becky and the kids are watching the sky for us now. Because the repairs to my radio were not finished at the airport, I can't give her a call." He circled the area again, coming in lower this time.

"Just what I thought—a sheet of water over the short grass. We dare not land there. But it's also risky to leave the airplane in an unprotected area. The only safe place is inside the hangar."

"You're right," the professor, a supervisor of Seventh-day Adventist church schools, agreed. "I've heard that several private planes have been hijacked in the last couple of months."

"The fuel gauge shows minimum reserves, and it's almost dark. With no lights, we must make a decision now."

David's favorite Bible promise flashed into his mind. "He who calls you is faithful, who also will do it." *Thanks, Lord,* he prayed silently. *Please help me make the right decision.*

"There's the road that parallels the hospital. It's high, dry, and seldom used this time of the evening." He circled the school until he saw someone waving. Then he scanned the road. *No vehicles in sight.* Dropping down toward the ground, he landed and parked the plane in a wide place at the side of the road. A teacher and the security guard soon arrived in a pickup truck.

"I'm glad you didn't try to land on the airstrip. Rain has poured all day," the guard commented. "I'll stay in the plane tonight. You can lock me inside."

"You can get out anytime you want to," David said. "Just turn the knob."

With fear in his voice, the guard exclaimed, "No, no, I don't want anybody to know they can get in or out. Nothing is safe in this part of the country."

"I'll be back early in the morning. Good night, and God be with you," David called.

He walked along the gravel road through the lush, green campus and gazed up at the darkening mountains in the distance. As he approached the driveway of his home, his two little girls squealed in delight, "Daddy, you're home!" One-year-old Carlos toddled on his chubby legs, hands outstretched. All smiles, their lovely blond mother ran to meet the man she loved.

"A king couldn't get a better welcome than this," David said joyfully as he hugged and kissed each one. Becky made sure everyone headed straight for the supper table. After David finished praying, Becky served the children and sat down next to David. She squeezed his hand and smiled.

"The sound of your plane landing always thrills me, and I breathe a prayer of gratitude to God."

"And I feel a kind of heavenly joy sitting here beside you, eating your delicious food and listening to the children chatter. After all the problems I faced out there today, this is peace."

After they finished eating, Becky suggested, "I'll clear the table later. Let's go to the living room and listen as Daddy tells us about his day." All three children climbed onto their father's lap, looking up with anticipation.

"I tried over and over again but failed to pull a young girl's infected tooth. The roots appeared to curve in and join together at the tips. It may be necessary to break the jawbone. When she screamed in pain, I promised I'd return as soon as possible with a dental surgeon. Her look of gratitude more than paid for the many other stops we made today."

Always sympathetic, little Lina interrupted. "I'm so sorry she hurt so much. I'll pray to Jesus to fix it."

"Thanks, honey. I'm glad you'll pray for her." David continued, "The professor and I visited several isolated schools that needed his help and were facing problems. We have a few more to visit tomorrow. I must get an early start because I need fuel."

"I see some sleepy little people," Becky remarked with a smile. "Time for all of us to go to bed. But the children see so little of their daddy, I told them they could wait up for you."

At 6:00 A.M. the next morning a couple of high-school students knocked on the front door of the Gates home.

"*Capitán,* there are soldiers around your airplane, and they want to see your documents."

"No problem. Tell them I'll be right there."

David turned to Becky. "I'm sure my documents are all in order. Let's see," he said, counting on his fingers. "I have a letter from the president of the country thanking ADRA for the work they do, plus my credentials from ADRA. I have permission from the director of civil aviation, one from immigration, and another from customs. Everything required to operate an airplane here is in order."

David turned to walk out the door, then stopped and came back to Becky. He joked, "Oh, I almost forgot to kiss you. In case I don't see you again, I want to give you a kiss." He was joking but held her tight for a moment. Becky said she didn't see anything funny about it. Then he walked outside and met the professor. With the students they drove in the school's pickup truck to the spot where he had left the plane.

"Good morning, gentlemen," David greeted the soldiers standing by the plane. "I understand you wish to see my documents. You will find everything in order." The soldier in charge, a captain, took the papers, looked them over carefully, and acknowledged that David was telling the truth. David noticed the name on his nametag, Gonzalez.

"Are you the pilot who was flying this plane two years ago?" Captain Gonzalez asked.

"No, I've been flying this plane for only a year and a half. The previous pilot left about two years ago. I'm David Gates." Captain Gonzalez appeared to be confused by his answer. Going back to their truck, the soldiers huddled and talked while the captain spoke on his radio. Then the soldiers returned to David and the professor. "We have to wait for instructions," the captain said. "Please stay right here."

"Gentlemen, I'm scheduled to make urgent visits to several villages today. I just received a telegram saying a man is dying and needs to be evacuated. I was also hoping to help a young girl with an infected tooth."

"Well, you can't move until the general gives the orders."

David felt impatient at the delay. He fidgeted and paced around the plane while the soldiers waited and waited. Turning to the captain, he asked, "Have you been here all night?"

"Yes, we have."

"Have you eaten supper or breakfast?"

"Neither," he answered.

David counted the soldiers. He called to one of the students standing nearby and said, "Please go to the hospital and bring back ten trays of food for these soldiers. They're hungry." The students climbed into the pickup and drove away.

A short time later they returned with breakfast for each of the soldiers. David stopped a passing truck and purchased a case of soft drinks. He handed one to each of the men. After they ate and drank, Captain Gonzalez smiled at David. "We had a good meal. Thanks a lot," he said.

Finally the soldiers heard the general's voice on the radio. Running to their truck, they listened for a few moments and then returned with the message, "The commanding officer wants you to fly to a special runway." David recognized the name of the place.

"But that's an abandoned runway," he said.

"That's where he will meet us."

A feeling of dread came over David, and he broke out in a sweat. Orders to land on an abandoned runway surrounded by armed soldiers! Something seemed terribly wrong.

"Sir, I prefer to land at the commercial runway just five miles from it. There's no reason for me to go there. You know everything's in order, so there's no problem."

"You'll be coming right back. Just a short stop for the general to check your papers." David didn't believe the captain. Getting more uncomfortable by the minute, he continued to resist.

Finally, one soldier stuck his gun at David's back and ordered, "Get in the airplane."

He knew he had no choice. Arguing wasn't going to work. The captain and another soldier climbed in the back of the plane, and the professor and David got in the front.

"I have a custom," David said, looking back at the two soldiers. "Before each flight I pray to the God of heaven for protection. Would you kindly remove your hats and close your eyes?" They complied as David prayed, "My Father in heaven, we ask Your blessing on each of the soldiers, on the professor, and myself. Please protect us from harm and evil with Your holy angels. I thank You in Jesus' name. Amen."

David took off from the road filled with apprehension. Because he had removed the two-meter radio to get it fixed, he had no way to inform anyone of his circumstances or destination. He would have given anything to talk to Becky.

As they flew he decided to act as if he were communicating over the radio. Putting the microphone to his mouth, he pretended to call the conference office. "Please advise Mexico City right away that we are headed for the abandoned airport. There may be some paperwork problems. Send a lawyer right away to deal with it."

Captain Gonzalez, sitting behind David, heard every word. He did not know that David was talking to a dead radio. David ended with, "Roger, roger, yes, we'll be landing in a few minutes. Please send a legal advisor immediately."

Still hesitant to land at the abandoned runway, David called back to the captain, "I'm going to land at the commercial runway."

"No, no, you can't. I have orders from the general that you must land as he instructed."

"But you told me that I'm going to be flying back home in a few minutes. I need fuel for I won't have enough."

"No," he spoke firmly, "orders are for you to land where the general said."

"Then you'll have to shoot me, won't you, because I am landing on the other runway." Captain Gonzalez began to act extremely nervous.

On the ground at the commercial airport, David filled the plane with gas. He overheard the general's voice shouting over the captain's hand-held radio. "Why did you let him land there?" the voice screamed angrily.

"The pilot refused to obey, said he needed fuel," Gonzalez explained.

David spoke quietly to the airport's air taxi operator. "Listen carefully. I am being hijacked. Call my wife or anyone at the mission hospital. Tell them I think I'll be held at the air force base." He felt confident someone would try to find him or make contact with the right people.

With the four men back in the plane, David took off and flew toward the abandoned airstrip. As soon as they landed, David felt a wave of swirling emotions. One soldier politely commanded, "Excuse me, leave the plane and stand over here. Please put your hands behind your back as

I handcuff you. Kindly stand against the wall while I blindfold you." Then David heard another command. "Put machine guns in their backs. If they move, just shoot them."

Is this for real? he thought. As he stood perfectly still, he could hear the soldiers noisily ransacking the airplane. Soon after, they placed David and the professor in the back of a pickup truck. Knowing the roads in that area, David could sense the turns in the route that took them to the air force base. He thought of John the Baptist, of whom the Bible says, "He came as a witness to testify concerning [the] light, so that through him all men might believe" (John 1:7, NIV). *Please God,* he prayed, *whatever is ahead, stay close and help me witness for You.*

The truck stopped, and the soldiers led them, still blindfolded, rapidly through long, narrow hallways with low doors. Fearful of banging his head, David ducked as low as he could. Finally they entered a room.

"Sit down," the rough voice of an interrogator ordered them. After a few minutes guards took the professor to another room while David remained. An interrogation began immediately. For an hour the soldiers questioned him, and then they placed David in the other room while they questioned the professor for an hour. The cycle repeated several times. David thought to himself, *This is part of a well-laid plan.*

Puzzled at the many irrelevant questions, David answered carefully, asking God for wisdom.

"You are all good people, aren't you?"

"Yes, we are."

"You wouldn't do anything illegal, would you?"

"Of course not."

"But you did distribute Bibles."

Knowing that the law barred foreigners from distributing Bibles, David had never done it himself, so he answered, "No, I have not. I am a registered nurse. I do medical work."

"Put down that he has distributed Bibles."

"If you put that down, I won't sign your document."

"OK, strike it."

The give and take of the interrogation lasted all day. Finally Captain Gonzalez stopped everything. His voice sounded kind. "You know, these men haven't eaten. They fed us a good breakfast this morning. The least we can do is give them lunch. Bring in the other guy. Take off their blindfolds and handcuff them in front. Can I get you chicken sandwiches?"

The professor answered, "Yes, thank you."

David added, "I don't want to appear picky, but you wouldn't mind making mine an egg sandwich, would you?"

"Not at all. Bring a chicken sandwich for him, and give the pilot an egg sandwich."

After a few bites of sandwich, David remembered the small piece of paper in his pocket listing contact information of friends and church leaders. In tiny print were many names, phone numbers, and addresses. In the wrong hands the information could be abused. He didn't want any Church officials arrested on false charges.

What should I do? I need wisdom, God, he thought. An idea popped into his head. He looked around the room. The soldiers were talking quietly among themselves. Reaching with both handcuffed hands into his pocket, he pulled out the small piece of paper, stuck it into his egg sandwich, and ate it. After he had chewed through the tough sandwich, he felt relieved.

When they had finished eating, blindfolded again and handcuffed behind their backs, the professor was pushed back into the interrogation room. The cycle of hour-long interrogations began again. Late in the afternoon David could hear the professor's answers for the first time. Someone had left a door ajar by accident.

"I hardly know *Capitán* Gates. Until just the other day we met for the first time. I don't know what he does."

David squirmed. The professor and he had worked closely together ever since he had begun his job as a mission pilot. *So he's buckling under fear and needs encouragement,* David thought.

When the soldiers brought David in for more questions, he spoke to the professor. "You have to tell the truth. If you start bending the truth, God cannot protect you. If they ever catch you telling an untruth, you'll hurt yourself. We know angels surround us. The soldiers can't touch us without God's permission. True, it appears we're prisoners now, but really, they're the prisoners and can only do what God allows them to do. Please don't be afraid to tell the truth."

The professor turned his face toward the interrogators and said, "I'm sorry. I should have told you the truth. I work with David Gates and know him well. For almost two years we've done everything together. Please correct my statement. I got scared." Captain Gonzalez struck it all out.

Then the blindfolds came off. David saw that a clerk had typed about twenty pages on an old typewriter. Nothing the soldiers had said gave David a clue as to why he'd been arrested.

"Read it and sign your name," the captain said.

David and the professor did as commanded. Then, blindfolded again, they were led by soldiers to the back of a pickup. David guessed they were in for a long ride over the mountains to the prison. He could tell when they were driving through town by the sounds around them. Just a few miles away, his precious wife and two little girls, Lina and Katrina, and their newly adopted boy, Carlos, waited for him. Now he knew how Joseph felt when the traders who were taking him to Egypt passed by the hills where Jacob, his father, lived. Why had God allowed this when David had prayed for wisdom and guidance? Did He have a plan to send him to a strange place as a witness to people who didn't know God, just as He had sent Joseph?

Confused and lonesome, David longed to be with his family. His heart began to break. Would he ever see them again?

CHAPTER 2

Time to Remember

Rain pelted down on David and the professor as they huddled close to the cab. The winding road and the low gears told David they were beginning a journey over the mountains. He had left home that morning in a short-sleeved shirt and without a coat. He could feel the cold wind clear through to his bones and began to shiver.

"You look cold, *Capitán,*" the guard said.

"Yes, I am kind of cold."

Taking off his jacket, the soldier placed it over the front of David's body and said in a kind voice, "Have my coat. You may keep it."

"Thank you so much," David said aloud. Silently he prayed, *Lord, these acts of kindness—being fed lunch, this man giving me his coat—they tell me that You are in command. Please give me discernment to show little acts of kindness to disadvantaged people I meet on this journey.*

Blindfolded, bumping along the winding mountain road that night, David had time to think. *No need to worry about what's ahead.* He would place that in God's hands. In the darkness and cold his mind focused on his beloved Becky. The years vanished as he recalled cherished memories.

David remembered what his parents had told him of the miracle God performed to save him as an infant. Born with intestinal atresia and malrotation (intestines intermittently closed and appendix on the left side), David had no peristalsis—no nerve action that would move food along. The physician came to his mother, Meraldine, who was then a nursing instructor at Washington Missionary College in Maryland (David's father, Richard, was studying at the seminary nearby) and said,

"Mrs. Gates, your firstborn son will die. He cannot possibly live, even though we tried to do restorative surgery."

During the first three weeks of David's life, the physician operated three times. He tried repairing the little intestines, but that didn't work. Later he removed a large section of bowel, but this did not bring a cure either. On the third try, he altered part of David's stomach, making a special connection to see if gravity would cause food to move down. Nothing seemed to help the infant, and no food passed through his intestines those first three weeks of life.

"We're so sorry, but we can do nothing more," the doctor said sadly. "Your child will die."

In faith David's parents asked Dr. Leslie Hardinge to anoint their baby. Within twenty-four hours a nurse began to hear bowel sounds for the first time. The doctor called for an X-ray of the baby's abdomen. Thrilled, the physician declared, "The appendix is now in the correct position. The intestines seem to be functioning normally, even though the baby was born without a working peristaltic nervous system." This agnostic physician continued, "If there is a God, He has spared this baby's life. I'm sure He must have great plans for him."

David, only a year old when his missionary parents took him to the jungles of Bolivia, grew up speaking Spanish. His father, a

David in Bolivia at ten years old.

pastor and mission pilot, took the family from the lowland jungles to visit the city of La Paz when David was three. The 14,000-foot altitude made the little boy sick. He still remembers his first glimpse of a pretty blond girl there. The girl's mother said to him, "David, this is our six-year-old daughter, Becky Sue."

Becky brought out games and puzzles, but before they played, she said with a smile, "Would you mind if I combed your messed-up hair?" Her motherly attention made him feel better.

Later she suggested, "Let's do finger painting. We can paint the mountains all covered with snow that we see out the window." Filled with all kinds of ideas, she kept him occupied until he forgot his headache and nausea.

Becky's father, Monroe Dale Duerksen, treasurer of the Bolivian Mission of Seventh-day Adventists, often visited the jungle lowlands, where David lived. He occasionally brought his family along. David happily suggested projects and Becky followed along. Tramping barefoot through the jungle, they collected flowers and caught colorful butterflies and unusual beetles. Sometimes they worked together on paint-by-number projects.

Becky, 15, with her monkey JoJo.

"We need to earn money to buy ice cream and gum. Got any ideas?" David asked one day.

"Let's each paint a picture of JoJo, my beautiful monkey," Becky suggested. That took a while because JoJo wouldn't sit quietly for his portrait.

When they were finished, David said, "I like our pictures of your pet monkey. Here's my idea. Let's find lids from cans, punch holes and put strings in the hole for a picture frame. We'll paste our monkey pictures and the best of our number paintings on the lid frames and sell them." The little entrepreneurs found many buyers as they stopped at the houses in the village.

The Gates and Duerksen families once traveled together on the mission launch, stopping to treat the sick at each village. David remembered having his fifth birthday on that trip. When the two were a little older, David and Becky loved to go fishing from the bow of the launch. He loved hearing Becky laugh as they threw the fish back into the water and watched them swim away.

"Let's build a tree house, " David suggested one day.

"But we can't climb up that high on the trunk," Becky objected.

"No, but let's bring the tree down to us and make a house in the branches. I know how to use an ax and a machete." With millions of trees making up the Bolivian jungle, the loss of one didn't bother the little builders. For three days they chopped until it fell. Going barefoot, they found it easy to climb up the now horizontal trunk to make a cozy tree house in the branches. But when the leaves dried up, they found their house less inviting and turned to other adventures.

The Mission purchased property in the lowlands, and the two families were involved in starting a cattle ranch. Here local students could work for a year to earn money to attend school. Becky's family lived in a small house. When David's family came to visit, all the kids had to sleep in one room.

"This is great," Becky giggled. "We can tell stories, and have fun before we sleep."

That night David slept in a hammock above Becky. With her foot she pushed the hammock, swinging him to sleep. Suddenly he got sick and vomited. Becky pretended to be asleep, fearing she'd be accused of making David sick.

When David reached the age of eight, he announced to Becky, "When I get big I am going to marry you."

"You are? OK, I'll be happy to marry you when we're old enough," the eleven-year-old girl responded.

Deciding he needed to give Becky an engagement present, David took his savings to a shop in the small town of Santa Ana. "I want to buy a bottle of perfume."

"You want perfume? Do you have a girlfriend already?" the store-keeper asked.

"Sort of," he answered matter-of-factly.

Pleased with his purchase, he gave Becky the pretty little bottle. A few days later Becky's brother, Jimmy, approached David. "You know what Becky does with that perfume you gave her? She puts it on her monkey after she gives him a bath."

David felt heartbroken—she was using his engagement gift on a monkey. He didn't understand girls, nor did he realize that this monkey was very, very special to Becky. For seven years she had taken it every-where she went, dressed it up, and loved it dearly. Every Friday after her bath, she'd bathe JoJo. When she put perfume on herself, she'd put it on him too.

When Becky turned thirteen, her parents moved back to the United States so that her father could study at Loma Linda University in Cali-fornia. During her high-school years, Becky jumped around to many schools in Louisiana, Arkansas, Kentucky, and Tennessee. David and Becky didn't see each other for many years. David never knew that Becky had not rejected his perfume love-gift. Many years later he learned her motive. She had shared her treasured gift with the animal she loved the most.

David's family left South America for Andrews University in Michi-gan when he was eleven. Later, they lived in Collegedale, Tennessee for ten years. David remembered the thrill he felt when he met Becky again. But time and circumstances had changed them, and he began to feel uncomfortable. Would she, a student at Southern Missionary College, have anything to do with a high-school kid?

In her heart, Becky knew she still had feelings for David. Each year on his birthday, she'd think of him and their long-ago promise to each other. Would they ever be together?

One Sabbath, the Gates family, who lived near the university, invited Becky and her roommate, Joy, for lunch. After they'd eaten David sug-gested, "I've got a cow to milk. Would you girls like to come with me?"

As they walked toward the barn David remarked to Joy, "Your long blond hair is so beautiful." Becky felt a twinge of jealousy and thought, *He's noticing her and not me!*

Right then she determined to let her short hair grow.

Neither David nor Becky ever mentioned the childhood promise. The differences in age and education seemed overwhelming, and each of them was dating someone else. Feeling sick at heart, David concluded that he no longer had a chance to marry Becky.

True, when they happened to meet, they would always visit briefly as friends. But even as they chatted Becky thought, *He's just a kid and has no interest in me now.* And David thought he was too young for her. It seemed to mean the end of those childhood dreams.

Suddenly David's pleasant reveries came to an abrupt halt as the pickup truck slowed down and stopped. He heard a gate creak and realized they had arrived at the prison. Captain Gonzalez took off the blindfolds and ordered them to come with him. David glanced at his watch. Three o'clock in the morning! The men chatted along the way almost like friends. The prison guard saluted as they entered.

"I have two prisoners for you," the captain said. "Put them in cell A, right there, but I don't want you to lock the cell door."

"Captain, what did you say? They're prisoners, and you say you don't want me to lock their cell door?"

"No, these gentlemen will not run away. I also want you to leave the door open. That's an order. Do you understand?"

"Yes, sir!"

As the captain left he called out, "Good night, gentlemen."

The guard walked over to David and the professor.

"I've been working here a long time," he said, "and I've never had a prisoner that I couldn't lock up. This is strange! But let me tell you one thing. Don't you set foot outside that door, or I'll shoot you."

As they lay down on their cots, David turned to the professor. "That's the third act of kindness since our arrest," he said. "Could the captain's actions mean that we are prisoners, but not really prisoners? Surely God's hand is behind this. I don't understand now, but I'm confident God has a plan. He called us, He's faithful, and we can trust Him. In His own time He will do it."

Prison Life

David and the professor remained in the cell for two days. To pass the time they shared Bible promises. Was God giving them a respite to strengthen them for what lay ahead or, like John the Baptist, prison time to prepare to bear "witness to the light" (John 1:8, NIV)?

"It will be interesting to see how 'God works for the good of those who love Him, who have been called according to His purpose,'" David said.

On the third day the guard commanded, "Come with me."

The pickup truck took them into the nearby town, to the district attorney's office. In a hearing room, various clerks were typing on their typewriters. An officer stood up and began to read the charges against David and the professor. Only then did they find out what had brought about the hijacking.

"You have been charged with several crimes involving the use of the airplane." David heard a long list of illegal activities—everything they could think of, it seemed. "You prisoners are accused of all of this," the speaker intoned.

David knew that he had never operated the airplane illegally. But the man in charge of the hearing gave them no opportunity to make a statement. David thought, *Looks like these government officials plan to stand at close range shooting a blunderbuss—scattering shot, bullets, and slugs at us all at once.*

"We have a witness to testify that the charges are true." David heard the name of a man who was also a prisoner. "He is willing to testify against you."

"Take them to prison," the officer shouted.

David remembered the witness's name and resolved to himself, *When we get to prison, I'm going to confront that man. I'll find out why he chose to testify about something entirely false.*

Back in the pickup truck, David saw that they were being taken to the federal prison. As they entered the prison, David again resolved, *I must find the man who accused me falsely.* The guard closed the gate behind them and fingerprinted them. From that moment, the thought of confronting his accuser disappeared from David's mind.

The guards took David and the professor to the inner prison. Immediately a crowd of other prisoners surrounded them. "So you are the big criminals!" they called out.

"What do you mean?" David asked.

In their hands they had the latest newspapers. The front-page headlines read, "Seventh-day Adventist Hospital Suspected of Using Doctors and Nurses and Aircraft for Illegal Activities. They Train Student Nurses to Commit Crimes. Ring Leaders Arrested."

David saw that it was a political ploy to bring dishonor to God's church. He turned to the prisoners and said, "Do you believe everything you read on the front page of the newspaper? Someone has lied. The truth is, we are missionaries for the Church."

"No, you're not. We know that you have money. We can see that you are well-dressed, which proves you have money like all criminals."

"No, we do not have money."

"Yes, you do. You must have lots of money."

"Sorry, guys, but you're wrong. We have never dealt in crime, and we have no money."

"Listen. We've got something to tell you," the spokesman for the prisoners shouted. "In this prison we prisoners run everything. We demand that you pay us money. Unless you pay money, you will be forced to clean up all the latrines twice a day."

"So?"

"You don't want to clean these latrines. You're obviously people of culture who would never do such a job."

"I'm a nurse. I'm a missionary of the Seventh-day Adventist Church. I am not too good to clean latrines."

"Mr. Gates, you don't want to clean these latrines. Feces float around everywhere. The plumbing is all messed up outside. Water comes in during the rainy season, and the contents float all over the bathroom. You have to scoop up all that mess every day. I'm sure you don't want to deal with that smelly stuff."

"I think you're misjudging me. I told you I'm a nurse and used to cleaning people's rear ends. Once I worked in a nursing home. It didn't bother me at all to clean up those old people. Try me out."

"No, Mr. Gates. We're going to give you a chance. We know you don't want to tackle that job. We'll give you two days to make up your mind. If you don't pay by then, you will have to do it."

"I can tell you right now. Please give me a bucket and a shovel, and I'll start work. In two days you'll get the same answer. I'm not paying you a centavo [penny]."

The professor interrupted David. "I disagree. Maybe we should pay."

David looked at him. "You're free to pay if you want. You have to make your own choices, but I don't mind doing dirty work. Mothers seem to have no trouble changing diapers. They don't enjoy the first messy diaper, but after two or three, they get used to it—no big deal."

That night the guards lined up the prisoners in five long lines. David and the professor were ordered to different lines. After each line had been counted, they ordered the prisoners into their respective cells, seventy men to a cell, and locked the gates.

In the cell, David saw long rows of cement beds with a three-foot space between each row, extending almost to the ceiling. The cell leader informed the new prisoners,

"You must pay three dollars for a bed or sleep on the floor."

Feeling stubborn, David decided that if he started paying for everything, the demands would never stop. They'd want more and more money all the time. Besides, the cement beds would feel just as hard as the floor.

"I choose to sleep on the floor," he said to the cell leader.

"Since you're a newcomer, you must sleep next to my bed," he ordered.

Knowing he slept soundly, David had to solve a new problem. He thought, *These guys would steal everything I have. What shall I do?* Since the cell felt hot and sticky, he decided, *I'll take my wallet, my keys, my hairbrush, and my pen and stick them in my shoes. Then I'll wrap my shirt around my shoes and use that as a pillow, sleeping only in my pants.* Having solved that, he lay down. The moment his head rested on the lumpy makeshift pillow, he remembered something important. He had forgotten to pray.

He got up and knelt down, expecting someone to throw things at him or shout obscenities. But nothing happened, so he began to pour out his feelings on his Friend.

"Lord, I need You. I don't know why You permitted me to go through this trauma. I hate this kind of treatment. I feel depressed and frustrated. You know how many people depend on our plane visits. Who will help them now? Who will do the work You have assigned me? It won't get done.

"Will the Church ever get the plane back? Why did You allow me to end up in this horrible place? What's Your reason for putting me here? I have to tell You how awful I feel. I know You're with me. Please help me survive this. Teach me to trust You. Give me wisdom to witness for You, even when I don't understand. Be with Becky and the kids, and in Your own time bring us together again. I love You though I'm miserable. I pray this in the name of Jesus who suffered so much more for me. Amen."

David lay down again. Then he heard a shout. "Hey, you! You religious or something?"

"Yeah, I am. I'm a missionary for God. I work for the Seventh-day Adventist Church."

"You believe in God?"

"I certainly do."

"Do you think God exists?"

"Yes. I know He exists. I know Him personally."

"Then answer my questions." David prayed silently for wisdom. Seventy pairs of ears listened as they talked. Soon another voice interrupted. Then someone else asked a question, then another, and another, for more than two hours. Over and over the Holy Spirit brought Bible texts to David's mind. In the dark these men bared their hearts and asked questions about a God that they longed to know. Everyone listened, fascinated. David knew that the Holy Spirit had arranged this captive audience.

The next morning David awoke and immediately knelt on the floor for prayer.

"Hold it, hold it, hold it," a young prisoner called and ran to him. "Do you mind if I pray with you?"

"No, not at all. Glad to have you." The two men prayed together, and David knew God was smiling.

The next evening as David knelt to pray, a third man joined him. Now God was listening to three of His children. Then it rose to four, five, six, seven, and up to eleven. God knew the longing in their hearts. He understood their desires to join His family. Could that be why He had sent David to be with them, to bring encouragement in this dismal place?

Many prisoners came to David privately and told him their stories. One man said, "I have a wife and children. I'm innocent. Someone set me up unjustly. I'm sentenced to serve ten years, and my wife and kids are suffering." Another man's eyes filled with tears. "I've done nothing wrong, but I must be here fifteen years, with no one to care for my family."

A wave of sadness washed over David. He knew he couldn't expect justice either. How long would he be sentenced to serve? And how would Becky manage with two little girls, ages five and three, and one-year-old Carlos?

In the three days after David's arrest, Becky had no idea where he was or if she would ever see him again. They were living on the border with Guatemala, and she remembered that another missionary, Lon Cummings, had been kidnapped. Had this happened to David? Had guerillas taken David to a jungle hideout? Were they torturing him? Would they demand a ransom or kill him? Horrible thoughts filled her mind as she pleaded with God, "Please, give him back to me."

During those days Becky felt as though her stomach were tied in knots. She couldn't eat. Standing on the bathroom scale, she saw that it registered one hundred pounds. That meant she had lost seven pounds in three days. She tried to force herself to eat, but the stress made swallowing almost impossible.

Knowing that she must hold up for the children's sake, she dropped to her knees and pleaded, "Lord, You must help me. I feel as though I'm going to fall apart. I need Your peace in this turmoil. I need it right now. You know how I love Your promise in John 14:27: 'Peace I leave with you, my peace I give unto you: not as the world giveth, give I unto you. Let not your heart be troubled, neither let it be afraid' " (KJV).

At that moment Becky felt God's peace wash over her. For a few hours she could function normally again. Then horrible anxiety came back to overwhelm her. She dropped to her knees and repeated the request, "Please, God, I need Your peace. I'm losing it." All day long and during her fitful nights, she claimed John 14:27 over and over again. She treasured that promise like a drowning person gasping for air.

Friends dropped by and asked, "Becky, how can you be so strong?"

"I'm not strong," she would reply. "I'm leaning hard on Jesus. Without His promises, I could not go through this, because I have no idea what's happening to David. But God knows. One thing I do know—God gives us special strength for special times."

One evening three-year old Katrina saw her mother crying. "Mommy, the angel can open the door."

Puzzled, Becky asked, "What door?"

"You know. Like Peter." Becky remembered that she'd read the Bible story about the apostle Peter's escape to the children several weeks before. She reached down and hugged Katrina.

"Pumpkin doodle, you have more faith than Mommy does. Thank you for reminding me."

Every hour Becky experienced the "fiery trial" Peter mentioned in his first letter (see 1 Peter 4:12, 13). She understood that God was allowing her to become a partaker of Christ's suffering. But during the suffering, she couldn't rejoice. Only by faith could she realize that someday she'd rejoice when His glory would be revealed.

CHAPTER 4

Thoughts of Becky

David knew many eyes were watching him as he prepared for bed the second night and two prisoners clasped his hands in prayer. As he lay down and silence filled the room, he felt the sweet presence of Jesus.

But sleep wouldn't come. He couldn't quit thinking. Airplanes had played a major part in his life, and now his thoughts turned to the one he had just lost—the reason for his arrest and imprisonment—and to other planes he had flown. He remembered how God had blessed him with his first airplane. Having flown often with his father as a boy, he longed to take flying lessons during his senior year in academy. Determined to find a way to get the money for lessons, he found a job at the college.

Soon he became a partner with two friends who owned an airplane. The long hours of work eventually paid off and he bought them out. Before he graduated at eighteen, he owned his own small plane.

One day, before David got his pilot's license, his father, an experienced bush pilot, took him for a flight in David's plane to the small paved airstrip at Georgia-Cumberland Academy in north Georgia. Pastor Gates practiced touching down twice, each time noting a combine cutting corn in the field next to the runway.

David wanted to try a landing himself. "That's too tight for you," his father cautioned. "I don't want you landing with that combine working so close to the side of the runway. I had to deviate sideways around it. I'm going to land and ask him to move off a little more before you take the controls."

David's father made a normal landing, but just after he touched down, the left landing gear folded and the left wheel dropped out from under the plane. The left wing dropped, and they shot out across the field. The combine, working in circles, appeared in front of them. Having no control over the plane's speed, Pastor Gates pushed the nose down and hit the combine head-on at seventy miles per hour. With this quick maneuvering, the plane missed the man driving the combine.

Then, deathly silence! When David and his father came to, blood was trickling down their heads and sliced arms. The shoulder harnesses had saved their lives. Both the airplane and the combine were badly damaged.

The doctor in a nearby emergency room patched them up. "Your injuries aren't serious, but it'll take time to heal," he told them.

During his recovery, David received a note from Becky, who had returned home for one semester.

"I'm so sorry your plane got wrecked," she wrote. "I've always wanted to learn how to fly and had hoped to learn in your airplane. I'm so glad neither of you are seriously hurt."

Because his plane was insured, David soon purchased a replacement. A dim hope flashed into David's mind. Could God be using the accident to work things out for good with this positive contact

The "Becky Sue" Cessna 140.

from Becky? Since his previous girlfriend had dropped him, he felt free to answer her note. Soon the letters became frequent.

A short time later Becky and her parents came to visit the recovering pilots. After they left, David's father said, "I've got news for you. Becky's mother told Mommy that Becky just broke up with her boyfriend because he had little interest in mission service, which is her life's goal. She hinted that Becky still talks of her childhood promise to you, David."

David's graduation from Collegedale Academy.

"Really, Daddy! For some time I've felt depressed about it, thinking I had no chance with Becky. This is great."

David reminded himself of the promise in Philippians 1:6. "Being confident of this, that he who began a good work in you will carry it on to completion until the day of Christ Jesus" (NIV).

He prayed, "Thank You, God. There's nothing too hard for you. If You want Becky and me to work together for You, please show me what to do."

Always quick to act, David shot from depression to feeling on top of the mountain. He wrote a letter to Becky, mailed it, but got it back four days later. In his excitement he had forgotten to put a stamp on it.

Their friendship developed rapidly. Becky drove down to attend David's graduation from Collegedale Academy. She felt so proud of him as he marched down the aisle. After the ceremony, she tried not to shiver as they stood outside in the cool breeze. Her heart skipped a beat when he slipped off his graduation gown and placed it gently over her shoulders.

Soon they began to talk about their mutual interest in missions. Becky had been studying medical technology at college. One evening as they walked on the college campus, David threw out a challenge to her.

"If we both want to be missionaries, we need to take nursing. Wherever God calls us, nursing skills can help people."

"But, David, I've always said that I will never be a nurse. Don't you think that our parents being nurses is enough of the medical profession in the family?"

David remained quiet, giving Becky time to think.

"I'm sure I'll never want to make nursing my profession," she continued slowly, "but if I don't have to work on a hospital ward, well, maybe the knowledge to help the sick would enhance our mission service."

"I'm not interested in making nursing my profession either, but only as a valuable tool to help people."

"All right, David, I'm willing. Let's go to the nursing department and sign up."

The nursing director shook her head. "I'm sorry. We have already accepted all the students we can take for this year. We could put you on the waiting list. You would be numbers seventy-eight and seventy-nine of those applying. You may take an exam, however, to ascertain your qualifications."

A few days later David and Becky returned to the nursing department to get their results.

"You did well," the director remarked. "You've been bumped up to seven and eight on the waiting list. Still, you're too far down the list to be accepted this year."

Three weeks later on the first day of college registration, David suggested to Becky, "I'm sure God wants this for us. Let's not sign up for a single class today, but wait and pray."

On the morning of the second day they asked again.

"I'm sorry. No chance."

Still the eager couple waited all day long, reminding God often that with Him all things are possible (see Mark 10:27).

"If this is God's will for us, He'll work it out. If not, He'll show us better plans," Becky said with confidence.

"Registration closes at four," David muttered, looking at his watch. "We have just five minutes left to register. Let's see if there are any developments." They approached the nursing advisors' table.

"Two spaces remain open, but we think the two girls will be coming," the nursing director told them.

"Registration has been going for two days, and they haven't shown up yet. I think I'm going to speak with the dean of students," David commented.

"If you wish," she responded, pointing to the dean's desk on the other side of the registration hall. David shared with the dean their desire to take nursing to be better qualified for mission service.

"We have a problem here," David added. "If we don't get into this year's class, we cannot wait for another year. We just won't take nursing. It's either now, or we will go on with our previous professions as planned."

"Come with me. We'll go speak to the director of nursing."

Approaching the director's table, the dean asked, "Is it true that there are two students on the list who have not registered or contacted you? If so, it seems reasonable this late in the day to let these two into nursing."

Just a few minutes after registration closed, David and Becky signed up and were accepted for a two-year nursing course. Becky turned to David as they left the registration tables.

"Isn't God great! Now we can study to be nurses together. I don't mind changing my major, even in my senior year. I know this is God's will."

The couple began doing everything together, but Becky felt they should wait for marriage until they had finished nursing school.

David objected. "Becky, you keep dragging your feet on everything. You simply won't move fast. Maybe I move too fast, but you keep pulling back on the opposite end. I guess you're the plow, and I'm the tractor."

"Could it be that God knows we need balance? I prefer to 'wait on the Lord,' and you're more like Paul, always running the race." She laughed, and David had no rebuttal.

A few months after classes began, they participated in a friend's wedding as bridesmaid and groomsman. During the reception a friend asked, "Are you two planning on getting married?" Becky's parents overheard the question and answered, "We think they'll be telling us any day that they plan to get married."

"What do you mean, 'any day'?" David interrupted. "Becky says she wants to wait until we finish college. How can we possibly think 'any day' when her plans are a year or two away?"

When David got home for Christmas that year, his father confronted him.

"Are you engaged yet?"

"No, Dad, I would never get engaged without talking to you first. I respect you enough to ask your opinion."

"Do you think you will marry Becky?"

"I am positive I will marry her."

"You're sure you have found the person you love and want to marry?"

"Oh, yes, I've found her. She's just what I want. We both love the Lord and have one great goal, to be missionaries and serve those who need help."

"In that case, you are basically engaged, even though you haven't officially asked her."

"Well, emotionally we're engaged. I belong to her, and she belongs to me."

"Mother and I have talked, and we've decided you are the ideal couple. God prepared both of you as you grew up in Bolivia. You've always been friends. But we're afraid for you. If your relationship grows more intimate and you wait too long, you might commit an error, which could destroy or at least scar your marriage. Or, in order to preserve your relationship, you might pull away from each other while waiting a few years. Either way we feel that it would be negative. So, if you want to get married, you have our blessing and permission."

Surprised, David realized that now, both sets of parents supported their going forward with marriage. Not wasting any time, David gave Becky a call. "Are you busy right now? It's such a beautiful day. I thought maybe we could take the Becky Sue for a spin."

"Sounds fun," she replied. "I'll meet you there." She smiled as she thought about him. How she loved his mischievous brown eyes, long eyelashes and crooked smile. When she began calling him, "Tall, dark, and handsome," he started calling her, "Short, blond, and beautiful." She still remembered the day he had excitedly taken her to see what he had christened his little Cessna 140. In big letters written on the nose of the airplane was the name, "Becky Sue."

Moments later, Becky arrived at the airport and found David doing preflight on the Becky Sue. "Be with you in a moment," he said with a smile. Quickly he finished and walked to her side. Tenderly he took her hands in his, looking deep into her blue eyes and said, "I know I asked

you once before, but I want to ask you again beside the Becky Sue …
will you marry me?"

Becky's face broke into a beautiful smile. "I'd love to marry you," she
whispered. David thought his heart would burst with happiness. "Let's
talk about the details as we fly," he suggested. He couldn't remember
where they flew. He just knew that this lovely girl sitting beside him
would be his forever.

As David turned the plane on final approach, the twilight sky, a
vivid red and orange, spread out around the setting sun. As they
reveled in the beauty before them, Becky exclaimed, "Look, God is
decorating the world to celebrate this special moment." Just before
they landed he reached over and kissed Becky on the cheek, their
first kiss.

"Don't you think you're a bit too fast?" she asked.

"Not at all," he said frankly.

"David, I suggest that you wait for the next kiss until Valentine's
Day."

"Poor suggestion," he said, smiling at her, "but since it's your idea I
have no choice."

They decided David must ask her parents' permission before the
engagement became official. So they drove all night, arriving at the hospital early on January 1, 1979. Her parents were working the night shift,
her father as a medical technologist, her mother as a nurse in the emergency room.

David found Becky's father first.

"What in the world are you doing here so early in the morning? You
were just here for Christmas."

David got up his courage and blurted out, "I'd like to marry your
daughter."

Dale Duerksen smiled. "Let me think about this." He paused, his
eyes twinkling. "Well, to tell you the truth, I've already thought about it.
I would be delighted."

The happy couple hurried to the emergency room, where Becky's
mother, Pat, worked. Engrossed with a difficult patient screaming at her
about an insurance policy that wouldn't allow treatment at that hospital,
Pat didn't see them.

They heard her tactful words. "We'd love to treat you, but your insurance won't allow us to do so. Please go to the hospital a couple of miles down the road and they will take care of you."

Suddenly Pat looked up and yelled, "Becky, David," and ran toward them. The woman kept on screaming until she noticed she was hollering at no one.

Pat suspected right away. "Are you two engaged?" she asked excitedly as she hugged them both. Their faces told her the answer.

Becky's sister, Betsy, and her fiancé, Ted Burgdorff, also a missionary who grew up in Bolivia, planned to be married shortly. The four of

Wedding day on the Gates farm in Apison, Tennessee.

them decided to have a double wedding under the trees in the gazebo garden near the pond on the Gates family farm near Collegedale, Tennessee. The roses, in full bloom, provided all the flowers. Becky's father, Dale, walked down the aisle with a daughter on each arm.

Lying on the hard cement floor of the prison cell, David envisioned his lovely bride again. He could almost hear his father's and his grandfather's words as they performed the ceremony. His heart beat faster as he remembered her sweet voice saying, "I do." On June 17, 1979, Becky became his partner for life. No longer did age matter, for he had just turned twenty and she twenty-three. They were one in Christ Jesus.

A loud snore jolted David from his reverie. The ugly reality hit him again. When would he see Becky again? How long would he be confined within these prison walls?

CHAPTER 5

Prison Challenges

On Sabbath morning David and the professor talked.

"We want to keep the Sabbath by worshipping God here in prison. He must have a special plan for us to celebrate Sabbath School together," David remarked.

"But how?" the professor asked. "You know we can't go to the prison officials and ask to have church services. They wouldn't allow that."

"I have an idea. Let's present another request."

Together they went to the head of the prison. "Sir, could we possibly do some medical work for the other prisoners?"

He looked interested. "How's that?"

"I'm a registered nurse. The professor here directs our church schools for all of southern Mexico. We would like to talk to the prisoners on health and education. Would that be OK?"

"Absolutely! Here, have the microphone." He handed it to David. "Make an announcement."

"Listen, everyone. At 9:30 we'll conduct a special meeting for all who would like to learn more about education and health. If you have any questions regarding health, we'll try to answer them. Please come."

"Thank you," said the prison director, and David handed him the microphone.

Later David discovered that God had performed a miracle that morning. Prisoners have a strict pecking order, and there was an unwritten rule that no one could use the microphone until he had spent five years in prison. But the prison director had bumped up David five years in that moment by saying, "You announce the meeting."

The prison held more than four hundred men. About three hundred fifty came to listen. The guards had never seen that many come to any meeting. Ready for trouble, they lined up along the back and sides of the room with their guns.

As David saw the men file in, he silently prayed, *God, You know I've doubted Your faithfulness in allowing the hijacking and our imprisonment, but right now I have a clue why You permitted this. We've never had this many join us in Sabbath School anywhere. I'm seeing You keep Your promise, "He will do it!" and perform another miracle. Use us during this worship hour to bring glory to Your name.*

They led the prisoners in singing several lively Christian hymns. The professor prayed and then shared the advantages of Christian education in southern Mexico. David followed, telling the story of God's plan for mankind, about creation with its perfect health and diet, and then the entrance of sin and evil and the degradation of mankind. Then he explained God's wonderful plan to restore people to His image. He showed how the eight natural laws of health would benefit everyone.

"If only Adam and Eve had listened to God instead of the enemy, we would still be in paradise. We'd have no need for prisons. Satan degraded mankind to sin and selfishness. Some of you are here because you're guilty of sin and living only for self. Others of you may be here unjustly because of the selfishness and hate of someone else. But there is hope for each of you if you will accept the unconditional love of God and Jesus Christ's free gift of salvation. Remember, He suffered and died in your place."

After David had explained the meaning of Calvary and the plan of redemption, he asked for questions. Hands shot up from every part of the room. Finally, at 1:00 P.M., he stopped. "Friends, we need a break for lunch, but if you wish to come back again this afternoon we'll continue." They returned in large numbers, and the program continued all afternoon.

When the meeting ended, men swarmed around David.

"I have had a severe pain here for days," one man said. "Can you help me?"

Another exclaimed, "I've been suffering from headaches for weeks."

"I feel nauseated and can't keep down any food."

"I have this growth on my eye and it pains me continually." The complaints kept coming.

Finally David said, "Let's go see the prison director. I can't examine you here. Maybe he has a suggestion."

The prison director said, "We do have a small dispensary. A doctor used to come to the prison to see patients, but that was a long time ago. If you can use it, do so. Come, I'll show you the place. It's empty now."

"I'm not a doctor, just a nurse. But if I can help someone, I'll be happy to try," David explained as they walked to the room. He looked around and found a few meager supplies but no medical books to which he could refer. "Maybe you can announce that I'll see patients tomorrow morning after breakfast."

From that day on David saw at least fifty patients a day. He soon realized that some of the prisoners had serious conditions that would require surgical intervention. The prison director allowed David to phone the medical director at the mission hospital near his home. Again David saw God's hand, because he could send word to his dear Becky. He wondered how she was facing this crisis at home with the children, and he longed to contact her directly.

The opportunity to speak with Becky came only once, at another time. After receiving permission to use the phone, David made a random call to a friend's house several miles from the hospital. Since the hospital had no phone, Becky had stopped in to see her friend Jane after she had finished shopping. Her main purpose was to inquire for any word about David. Moments after Becky entered the house, the phone rang. It was David calling from the prison.

David longed to share with her the dark cloud of despair that hung over him. "It looks as if I'll be here for fourteen years, so you may have to move over here so we can be together on visiting days," he told her.

"Would you be kept on salary for the next fourteen years?"

"I don't know, but at this point the legal director tells me it could come to that."

"David, I must tell you what happened last night. The girls were in bed with me listening to their bedtime story about Peter's escape from prison. Katrina asked, 'Mommy, don't you think Jesus can unlock the prison doors for Daddy just like he did for Peter?'

"I answered, 'Yes, He can.'

"She asked, 'Don't you think we should pray tonight that Jesus will do the same for Daddy?'

"I said, 'I think we should.'

"She asked, 'Will He do it?'

" 'If that's His will,' I assured her. But, David, as we prayed He poured over me a tremendous peace. I knew that God is a living Presence encouraging both you and us with His protecting love."

The phone conversation lasted only a few minutes, but it meant the world to both of them.

At the mission hospital, the physician made arrangements for conducting surgery at the prison. The next day he made the long trip over the mountains from the hospital with surgical packs. He had no trouble getting into the prison.

"Hi, Dr. Mauricio," David greeted him. "You have no idea how happy I am to see you."

"*Capitán,* I can't stand to see you behind prison bars. You don't look the same."

"I'm not the same."

The guard immediately began to search the surgical packs. As he opened the first one David shouted, "You can't open those sterile packs. You'll contaminate them and ruin the sterility."

"We have orders that we must search every package that comes into this prison."

"Hold it right there. Quick, call the prison director, " David said firmly.

David explained to the director, "Sir, the guards can't open these packs. The doctor brought them from the hospital to do surgery. They must keep them sterile so the patients will not get an infection."

"Don't open any more," the prison chief ordered. "Anything Gates brings in, you don't open at all. Is that clear?"

"Yes, sir."

All of the equipment and packs went directly to the dispensary. The doctor, with David assisting, performed fifteen minor surgeries that day and more the following day. A few men needed major surgery, for which the doctor made arrangements with a local surgeon.

Because of the doctor's visit, the Adventist Community Services office received permission to bring clothes into the prison. Women from the nearby churches, when they heard that the missionary pilot had been put in the prison, brought meals of rice, vegetables, and fruit. David and the professor couldn't eat all the good food brought to them. David asked the director, "Please, may we have permission to distribute food to other prisoners?"

Many came eager to receive. One man whispered to David, "I belong to your church. May I have some of your food?"

"Of course you can. But I do have a question for you. Does that mean you eat only fish on Fridays?"

"Yes."

"And you only eat pork on Saturdays?"

"Yes."

David laughed. "Next time, please don't lie to me. You don't have to belong to my church. Anyone who needs food may have it no matter what church he attends. You may have food anytime, but please tell the truth."

The prisoners, locked up in the cell from six at night until six in the morning, did enjoy a kind of freedom during the daytime. In the mornings wives and families could meet them in the prison yard. Some brought in food to cook and sell to other prisoners. David looked for and found positive things about this prison, so much so that he wrote a letter to the prison director.

Dear Sir,

I am impressed with the way you conduct this prison. You have a prison board that includes your most respected prisoners, who may participate in the discipline within the prison. You invite the prisoners' families to come in. The children have the privilege of being with both their parents during the daytime. I doubt this ever happens in the United States.

I understand that the U.S. Embassy has sent word to you that if I am convicted I can serve my sentence in the U.S. I don't intend to serve any sentence, here or in the States, but that's God's problem, not mine. Whatever happens, I choose to stay in Mexico where I could see my wife and children every day. It is good that you also allow conjugal visits twice a week so that the wives of senior prisoners may stay overnight and the wives of junior prisoners can visit during the day.

I also appreciate the organized volleyball team. It provides good exercise and a chance to forget for a few hours that one lives in prison. The other prisoners appreciate my height and ability and have begged me to stay in prison to help their team win. I choose not to accept that invitation.

You have done much to make prison life bearable. Thank you.
David Gates

A few prisoners would routinely bribe the guard to let their girlfriends in on Tuesday and their wives on Thursday. Shortly before lockup time one afternoon, David heard a loud racket and screaming, along with laughing and clapping coming from the prison yard. He joined others to look out the window to the yard. They saw a naked man running around the yard being chased by a woman who was hitting him on the head with her high-heel shoe. The onlookers shouted in glee, "Give it to him, lady! Let him have it."

The guard had made a mistake. He had allowed the prisoner's girlfriend inside but forgot about her when the man's wife came in later. She found her husband busy with the girlfriend, grabbed her shoe, and began beating him. He ran around and around while she shouted and clobbered him, to the delight of the cheering prisoners.

David found the dull monotony of most of prison life hard to bear. Every day seemed an eternity. His active nature stagnated in prison. However, the medical work continued. David realized that this work not only relieved the pain of the prisoners but also his own heartache. He asked himself, *Could love be an action even if I feel angry and hurt?* At least, he consoled himself, the prison committee had never demanded that he clean latrines.

During the first few days of imprisonment he noticed an elderly white-haired man watching him. He looked like an American but spoke beautiful Spanish. One day the man approached David.

"Hi. My name is Donovan. I heard you're in for criminal offenses," the man said.

"That's what I'm here for," David replied, "but not what I'm guilty of doing. I'm actually a medical missionary."

"You are? What church do you belong to?"

"Seventh-day Adventist."

"Where did you learn Spanish? You speak it like a native."

"I was raised in Bolivia."

"Oh, you grew up in the Inca Union," the man said with a knowing smile.

"Wait a minute! How do you know about the Inca Union?"

"My missionary parents raised and educated me as a Seventh-day Adventist. My father and I opened the work of God in Colombia. See this scar of a bullet hole in my leg? A mob, led by a priest, objected to my father and me sharing our faith. They stormed the church and began to slice people as they ran out the door. My dad had machete cuts on his back, but we both escaped. The other missionary with us didn't make it. They cut him up into small pieces, threw the pieces into a gunnysack, and tossed it on the steps of the church with the message, 'This is what we do with all foreign missionaries.'

"I lived through violent times. In many of the countries of South America, the missionaries faced great difficulties and horrible persecution. In spite of all this I chose to enter mission service. I studied theology at Pacific Union College. Later I finished a master's degree and a Ph.D. in education. When Antillian College first opened in Cuba, they appointed me the director. My father was the secretary of the South American Division."

"I know your brother," David interrupted. "When my parents and I worked in Bolivia, he used to mail our monthly paycheck from the Division office."

"Yeah, he worked there as associate treasurer."

Filled with compassion, David asked gently, "Then, why are you here in prison?"

"Well, I allowed myself to get bitter toward the Church. I walked out on my wife and family. For some years I did tourism but then got involved in drug trafficking. For ten years I supervised the loading of airplanes with drugs and sending them out of Colombia. I was caught in Mexico and sentenced to thirteen years. I've served about nine of them."

"Now I know why God sent me here," David exclaimed. "God brought me here for you."

"But I have chosen to never look back. I wish I could, but I can't."

"Donovan, God wants you to look back now. He placed me here, a missionary kid from South America just like you, so you can see the big picture. You've given up your family, your wife, your children, your home, and your God. You're a hurting, lonely man, but you can find peace in coming back to God. Have you formed a new home?"

"Yes, I have a wife from Costa Rica, and two children that come to see me in prison every day. I don't want my children to be like me and experience what I've been through."

"Are they in school?"

"Yes, they attend public school, but I wish they could go to church school and also attend church. Could you help me?"

"Absolutely. I can make arrangements for you. I'd like to meet your wife and two children."

David talked with Donovan's family when they visited the prison the next day. With the help of church members and conference leaders, David arranged for scholarships for the children to attend church school. Soon they began to attend Sabbath School.

Often the two men met to visit, pray, and study God's Word. Over and over the prisoner queried, "Is God still interested in me after all the things I have done? What is God's will for me now?" David flooded him with hope and assurance from the Word of God. God took back His wayward son and wrote "forgiven" over every one of his sins.

For David the inner struggle increased. Each day in prison added weight to the deep, heavy cloud that smothered him. The South Mexican Union had acted quickly, sending their legal director, Pastor Hayasaka, to try to get the two men released. However, he brought little hope.

After many hours of futile attempts to get the two prisoners released, the legal director came to the prison requesting to see David and the professor.

"I'm sorry to tell you, but I fear we can do nothing," Pastor Hayasaka told them. "The military is determined to keep your airplane. To do so, they will do anything, even if it means keeping you in prison. At the time of your sentencing they will probably manufacture evidence proving your guilt. After they have verified all the accusations with witnesses and have proved you guilty with evidence, there is no way to get you released. Over and over, I've asked for permission to get into the courthouse to see your records, but they refuse. I can't find a single Catholic lawyer who will defend a Protestant. I fear there's no defense for you in this town."

He continued, "I have only one hope. I've heard of a Nazarene, the only lawyer in town who might take a Protestant. Reports say he is well respected, but no one will tell me where I can find his office. I have walked and inquired for days and can't even find a clue. I've been praying much. Now I've come to pray with you men. Only God can help in this desperate situation."

"For with God nothing shall be impossible," David quoted as they knelt together.

CHAPTER 6

The Cloud Begins to Lift

The prayer session filled Pastor Hayasaka with courage and faith. He began his search for the Protestant lawyer early the next morning. He walked and looked and asked everyone he met. No one would give him any information.

After several hours he paused in a quiet place to plead with God. "Precious Lord, I can't look any further. If you want me to find the Nazarene lawyer who would defend *Capitán* Gates and the professor, You must lead me to him. I don't know where to turn. Please give me Your divine guidance."

The director opened his eyes and looked above his head. He saw a small sign that said "Notary Public." He knew that in Latin America such a title always indicated someone who was a lawyer. He walked into the office.

"I am looking for a Nazarene lawyer in this town. Could you please tell me where he is?"

"Why did you come into this office?" asked the secretary at the desk.

"I've been looking for hours and stopped to rest. I saw that sign," he replied, pointing to it. "So I walked in here, the first office. Could you please tell me where he is?"

"Yes, I can tell you. Few people know this is his office, but he is upstairs right now."

Breathing a prayer of gratitude, Pastor Hayasaka followed her up the stairs and into the lawyer's office.

After introducing himself, Pastor Hayasaka explained the details of the case. The lawyer said, "Yes, I'm interested in helping these men. Let's go to the courthouse and examine the records."

At the courthouse, the attorney studied the records for some time. "I can find no evidence at all for conviction. Both men answered all the questions by saying the right thing. Even if I had been sitting by their side, I couldn't have helped them answer differently than they did. God certainly gave them wisdom during their interrogation. However, if the government does produce evidence, we will have a fight on our hands. I know of no way that the defense can prove that their evidence is totally false. If they produce any evidence of what they say they found in the airplane, and witnesses who swear they took it from the plane, how will we, on the defensive, prove these two men are innocent?" He paused, shook his head, and suggested, "Let's pray together, asking God for wisdom. "

The medical work in the prison continued, with David treating many patients each day. Outwardly he appeared to be a loving Christian nurse, happy for the opportunity to serve God by caring for the needs of those who were hurting. Inwardly he struggled with negative thoughts, depression, and discouragement. Thoughts of "what do I care about how you feel?" welled within him.

A patient would complain, "I'm hurting right here."

"I'm having this drainage."

"I'm unable to sleep at night because of back pain."

Covered with a cloud of despair, his emotions boiling inside of him, David thought, *Big deal! Don't you think I have bigger problems than you do, buddy?*

He struggled in vain to shake this attitude. Finally he concluded that love isn't always an emotion. Christian love is an action. He could listen to them. He could care for their needs. Though he didn't feel like a loving Christian, he could express sympathy. He could rely on God to show compassion that he didn't feel.

Inwardly, he longed for freedom. He wanted to be with Becky and the kids, to flee from treating prisoners' physical needs. In desperation he prayed, "God, all I can do is rely on You to change my attitude. Meanwhile, give me the fruits of the Spirit to continue to work as Jesus did. I know You want me to relieve suffering. Give me the mind and love of Jesus."

After he prayed this prayer, David marveled at the way God gave him the power to be patient when he felt impatient. Day after day he sensed God's presence, stooping down to teach him the lesson of trust. Previously David had used his clever mind to solve most of his own problems and difficulties. Now he felt powerless. He could do nothing except submit to God.

Finally he made the hard decision of complete submission. "Lord, even if I'm here for fourteen years (oh, I hope You don't keep me here that long), I'm willing to trust You. I prefer to be released from prison, for You know I'm innocent of the crime for which I'm accused. But if You don't arrange freedom, I will still trust You completely. I've barely started my missionary career, but if this is to be my mission for the next fourteen years, I choose to trust You no matter what.

"And, God, if this is a training period like the one You granted Moses for a future work, so that I may learn patience, dependence on You, and unwavering trust, then so be it. Thank You for whatever You plan for the future. I'm not afraid as long as my hand is in Yours."

God put two thoughts into David's mind. " ' "Do to others what you would have them do to you" ' (Matthew 7:12, NIV), even if you don't feel like it." And "when you 'cast your bread upon the waters, for after many days you will find it again' " (Ecclesiastes 11:1, NIV). His treating the soldiers kindly the day the plane was hijacked resulted in kind treatment to him. Treating the prisoners' physical and emotional needs could result in changed attitudes. The Spirit whispered, "God loves to turn blessings given into blessings received. Each time we give, we get much more."

Later, David heard through the grapevine that the prison director had noticed the long hours he spent giving medical aid to prisoners. Surprised at the clothes and food brought in by the church, and amazed that the Adventists paid for a doctor to drive over the mountains to do minor surgeries and later arrange for a local surgeon to care for serious cases, the director felt impressed to act. He decided to make a visit to the district attorney and share what he had seen.

"You say these Adventists are criminals," said the director to the district attorney. "Let me tell you something! This is the best thing that ever happened to our prison. They continually do medical work, helping all the prisoners. They sent a doctor from over the mountains to do surgery. They bring in clothes and food, and help our prisoners in any way they can. If you don't drop those charges, I shall be forced to publish an article about the Adventists and the good work they are doing in our prison."

Hmmm, the district attorney thought. *I dare not let that be published.*

Suddenly the DA summoned the Adventist legal director, whom he had shunned before. Looking up from his desk, he spoke abruptly.

"We're willing to drop the charges against your men."

"You are?"

"Yes. Instead of a major crime, we will accuse Gates of being involved in a misdemeanor."

"Why do you want to do that?"

"You can defend yourself easily on that account. There's no evidence to prove that's true. Your men can get out on bail and go home."

In many Latin American countries, legal proceedings are accompanied by demands for cash. The legal advisor asked, "How much will it cost me?"

"Five hundred dollars for the official bail and five hundred for 'other' expenses!"

He went immediately to the conference to obtain the money. Even before he returned with the money, the authorities had released the professor.

Not knowing the reason for the professor's discharge, David felt overwhelmed as he watched him go. Smothered with discouragement, he complained to God. "So they choose to release their own man and keep the American in prison. We're both innocent. God, this isn't fair. How long will You leave me here to learn the lessons of submission and dependence on You? May I rest in Your love as You give me perfect peace."

CHAPTER 7

The Long, Long Night

Sleep would not come as David tossed and turned on the cement floor of the cell.

He prayed over and over again. "Why, Lord? Is this Your plan for me?" He seemed to hear again, "In God I trust; I will not be afraid. What can man do to me?" (Psalm 56:11, NIV).

"I'm sorry, Lord. I know You are with me, and I do trust that You will bring Your plan to pass. Help me to think happier thoughts."

Again his thoughts turned to Becky and the early years of their marriage. He remembered the team spirit he and Becky developed as they finished nurse's training and became RN's. Her encouragement enabled him to complete his professional aviation training. Since they had received no call to mission service, they accepted an invitation to join David's parents in Pucallpa, Peru, as volunteer missionaries with no salary. For six months they worked with the jungle people.

David smiled as he remembered the prayer they prayed one day: "God, please give us an idea of how to support ourselves and continue in Your missionary work."

The next day David saw a man in the village wearing a hat with the words "In Gold We Trust" sewn on it. He hurried to the man and asked, "Where do you get gold around here?"

"In the river."

"Could you show me how to do it?"

"Sure, no problem. It's hard work, but there's gold for anyone who is willing to put in the time." David couldn't wait to tell Becky.

"I think that would be kind of fun to do. With God's help we could make enough for food, and also medicine for the sick."

So David and Tim, another volunteer worker who maintained the aircraft at Pucallpa, decided they would try this adventure during their two weeks' vacation. That would be enough time to experience life as gold miners, they decided. Becky and Jenny, Tim's wife, remained at the airbase in Pucallpa.

The would-be miners lived on a river beach far from the small town of Puerto Inca and dug every day. All day long they washed the dirt and panned for gold. This experiment convinced them that with God's help and lots of hard work, they could pan enough gold to buy medicines and food.

The two wives, lonesome for their husbands, decided to visit them.

"Is there any possibility that on one of your next mercy flights, you could drop us off where David and Tim are working?" Becky asked her father-in-law.

"Sure can. I'm going near there on Thursday."

David remembered the joy he felt as he saw his lovely wife step out of that plane. That night they spread their sheets on the sand. Sleeping accommodations consisted of a plastic tarp over their sleeping bags. Since it hadn't rained for three months, they had no worries. But during the night the weather changed and rain woke them up. In moments the gentle drops turned into a drenching tropical rain.

Becky wadded up one of the blankets and huddled over it for hours. At least it stayed dry. The guys kept dumping the water from the plastic tarp, but soon they were all soaked.

Finally the rain stopped, and all four of them huddled under the one dry sleeping bag. What a miserable night! The next day, Friday, the girls washed the wet, sand-covered sheets and blankets in the river and spread them out to dry.

A farmer named Emerson and his helpers came by in his long canoe. He stopped to talk. "Do you think the river will rise any higher?" David asked.

"No, you don't need to worry. That's probably all it will rise," he replied.

Tim and David talked about where they should sleep that night. "We'll construct a nice little shelter off the sand in the grass. That way we can be sure we'll have a good sleep and can enjoy a happy Sabbath together. It's easy to get balsa wood in the jungle. We can use the plastic tarps for a slanting roof."

The finished shelter pleased them all. "Let it rain, doesn't matter anymore," David exclaimed. "We can stay dry in our cozy shelter at the edge of the woods."

Extremely tired from lack of sleep the night before, they went to bed early that Friday night. The clear sky seemed to assure them of no more rain. But about 2:00 A.M. they awoke with a floating sensation. David reached out his hand and plunged it into several inches of water.

"Oh, no!" he exclaimed. "The river must be rising fast. Heavy rain must have fallen upriver in the mountains." In the darkness they grabbed all their stuff and waded toward the hill, stumbling and falling over tree roots. But the river kept following them. It rose twenty-five feet that night. They hung what they could in the trees and returned for more trips to get their food, their generator, and other equipment that would float down the river if not retrieved quickly. Another miserable night!

The next morning, after a skimpy breakfast of the little food that wasn't soaked, they decided to enjoy Sabbath School together in the woods. Later, Emerson, who had assured them of no rain, came by on the river with a boatload of men, and he saw their little house floating in the water, but no sign of people.

Oh, no! he thought. *What happened to the gringos? I told them the river wouldn't rise, and it did.*

Emerson beached his boat, and the men began looking for the missing missionaries. When they heard singing, they followed the sound and found them. With a big smile he suggested, "Please, let me take you to my house. All your clothes, bedding, and food are wet."

"We'd rather not move all this equipment on the Sabbath, because this is our day of rest. We never do work like that on Sabbath. We would prefer to come tomorrow. I think we can manage here."

"I understand. You are Seventh-day Adventists and can't work on Sabbath."

Turning to his men, he ordered, "Pick up their stuff and load the canoe."

Almost immediately, eleven men had picked up all of their baggage and equipment and deposited it in the canoe. David smiled as he said to Becky, "Looks like all our menservants are doing the work, while we keep Sabbath holy."

Emerson took them to his comfortable home built on a hill far above the river. His friendly wife, Lina, welcomed them as she quickly provided a delicious meal and a comfortable place to sleep. Both couples enjoyed the hospitality of this lovely Catholic farmer. This friendship later proved to be a great blessing to David and Becky.

They discovered that working among the villagers in that isolated area of Puerto Inca was very rewarding. Medical care led directly to spiritual interests.

With medical supplies and food frequently running low, David and Becky saw the need for an airplane to fly into the many small villages to care for the sick. One day David surprised his wife with an idea.

"Sweetie-pie, let's go to the States and work as nurses at Madison Hospital in Tennessee until we earn enough to buy an airplane. If we make a pact with God to do everything possible not to work on Sabbath, I know He will bless."

"I do not want to do what I've seen other nurses do, work overtime on Sabbath just to get more money. If we have to care for the sick on God's day, I'll do it willingly. But all that money earned on Sabbath belongs to God. Maybe we can get them to schedule us from Sunday to Thursday whenever possible."

With that resolution in their minds, David and Becky moved back to Tennessee and began working in the hospital. God blessed them financially, but they had to pay a price for this resolve. The supervisor scheduled them to work on a different floor almost every week.

"We do not allow family members to work together on the same floor," the supervisor told them. "Past experience has proved that they don't get along well."

One day in an emergency, the staff had no choice but to put the couple together.

They found that David and Becky made a harmonious team. After that Becky felt the thrill of the smiles and sweet words David whispered as they passed each other in the hospital halls. Yes, lovers can continue their romance even at work. After six months at the hospital, they had saved enough to buy a Cessna 150 airplane.

They had a great time getting the plane ready for the long flight to the mission field. David and a friend flew the small airplane to Peru, and then he returned for Becky. He remembered her saying, "This is just another honeymoon. What fun we have together!"

When David and Becky returned to Peru with their airplane, Emerson, the kind Catholic farmer who had taken them into his home, gave Becky and David a little house to live in. The close contact generated a precious friendship with this family. Becky and David would eventually name their firstborn baby girl Lina, after Emerson's kind wife. This industrious, hardworking man inspired them to live their faith as he did. He and his four sons gave food and medicine to anyone around them in need, putting into practice the principle Jesus gave in Matthew 25:40: " ' "Whatever you did for one of the least of these brothers of mine, you did for me" ' " (NIV).

Knowing the need for more medical work, Emerson sold a choice piece of land to David and Becky. Later David sold the property to Becky's parents, who, with their medical skills, developed a thriving clinic. Working there for seven years, they treated 28,000 patients. This came about because of the kindness of a local farmer who cared.

Lying on the cement floor in the dark, David shook his head. He was now a professional pilot of many years' experience, and he marveled at God's loving protection. *We kept the angels busy while we flew that little underpowered, two-seater airplane all around those jungles in Peru, landing on poor airstrips,* he thought. *What joy we had bringing food and medicines to isolated workers and taking patients out for treatment. Very few people know this joy. They fear to venture forth without money.*

While he was flying over the jungle of Peru one day, God had impressed David that he must learn to do his own airplane maintenance. "Sweetie-pie, to be effective, we need to return to the States for more training. When something goes wrong with the plane, I need to know how to fix it. Good mechanics aren't found in the jungle."

The couple moved to Kentucky so that David could study aviation maintenance for two years. With Becky pregnant and neither of them able to find part-time nursing jobs, they learned that education sometimes requires a high sacrifice. During the first few months they lived in a small camping trailer in a state park. The second year both found jobs at the Adventist hospital in Manchester. Two daughters, Lina and Katrina, were born there.

Shortly before finishing his course of studies, David and a friend were working on an airplane. In his hand he held a pair of needle-nosed pliers, and his partner said, "Pull up with all your might." David pulled hard on the wire, and it slipped. Unable to stop himself, he drove the pliers into his left eye with both hands. He saw a flash of red and fell on his knees. Instantly, he thought that his flight career was over. He expected to feel fluid running down his cheek. But no, he felt it, and his cheek was dry.

However, he couldn't see anything with that eye. Reaching up fearfully, he pushed his finger on his eye, expecting that it would go all the way in. Instead he felt pressure. "Oh, Lord, I can't believe it. The eye must still be there."

He ran to the bathroom and looked into the mirror. Aloud he exclaimed, "I can see a big hole in my eyelid. The needle-nose pliers bounced off my eye, went on the inside of my eyelid, and came out the other side without causing serious damage to the eyeball."

David now remembered his prayer of dedication. "Lord, You saved my life as a baby. Now You have saved my eyesight when I'm older. Nothing that I have can ever be considered mine. If You ever allow me to fly in the mission field, if You ever give me opportunities to serve overseas, I dedicate everything I have and my whole life to You again. If I lose my life, that is Your problem. You've already given it back to me so many times. You've returned what I should have lost. What You have restored belongs totally to You."

Having completed his missionary preparation as a professional pilot, aviation mechanic, and RN, David grew concerned as he watched denominational aviation programs closing around the world. He realized he needed to diversify his education. "Sweetie-pie, the economic and political situation may soon close the Church's aviation program in Peru. Computers are coming into prominence. Skilled computer programmers and operators are in high demand. To ensure that I will be needed in the mission field, I need to complete professional training in that area." So David continued his studies in the United States, while he and Becky supported themselves by nursing. He obtained a bachelor's degree with a specialty in computer science. David began work on a Master of Science specializing in software engineering. Through a combination of correspondence courses, distance education, and classroom instruction over six years, he would eventually complete the course of studies and return to the U.S. for graduation.

Now that David was much more qualified, officials of the General Conference of Seventh-day Adventists Secretariat informed him that three countries were asking for his services—Brazil, Peru, and Mexico. Which one would be God's choice for him and Becky? Which one had the greatest need?

"We need Your help, God," they prayed. "Remember Your promise, 'He who calls you is faithful, who also will do it.' Friends urge us to consider the advantages in both Brazil and Peru. But we just learned that the twenty-two-bed hospital and nursing school in southern Mexico needs an administrator who could assist the medical and dental students who volunteer each year from Loma Linda. This requires a pilot to fly their airplane to the many villages in the area to bring supplies and give counsel to these young workers. Are we qualified for such responsibilities?"

"Another request, God," Becky added, "the South Mexican Union says they now have no budget for an overseas base deposit, and no benefits in the States. We must live on the local salary of only $300 a month. With two little girls to care for, is this Your plan for us? I have faith in Philippians 4:19, 'My God shall supply all your need according to his riches in glory by Christ Jesus' " (KJV).

And so they turned down the more lucrative calls, trusting God to lead and guide them in southern Mexico.

Lying on the floor of the prison cell, David recalled many of the challenges and joys God had given them over the year and a half they had served in this needy area. Little Carlos, their adopted Mexican boy, brought them tremendous joy. But if God had led them, why had He allowed the airplane to be hijacked and David to be condemned to prison, perhaps for fourteen years?

With these troubling questions racing through his mind, David began reminding himself of God's precious promises. *We know that in all things God works for the good of those who love him, who have been called according to his purpose* (Romans 8:28, NIV). *"For nothing is impossible with God"* (Luke 1:37, NIV). *"So do not fear, for I am with you; do not be dismayed, for I am your God. I will strengthen you and help you; I will uphold you with my righteous right hand"* (Isaiah 41:10, NIV).

"That's enough, God. I know I can trust our future in Your hands. Thank You for the peace of submitting all to Your love and power."

With his troubled mind at rest, David slept soundly.

Home Again!

In his despair, David had forgotten the special significance of the next day. But God hadn't forgotten. God had chosen to keep the American in prison one more day to give His beloved children a surprise.

On that day, the legal advisor gave the district attorney the money for David's release. The DA stuffed it into his pocket. Then, going to his desk, he signed the paper, handed it to the legal director and said, "We've dropped the charges. Now go pay the bail and get Gates out."

Only then did David realize what a small price he had paid—ten days of medical work for a lifetime of freedom. He rejoiced that he had not yielded to the temptation of depression and had not refused to do his best to help others. Until his release he had not understood God's method of handing him the keys to the prison. He had served others in ignorance, not knowing that this medical work would unlock the prison doors for him.

As the guards led David out of prison, they stopped him to sign out. He walked through the gate and heard it slam shut. At that moment David remembered hearing the same sound on the day he entered the prison. Suddenly he realized it was that moment when he had determined to contact the man who had falsely testified against him. During those ten days he had completely forgotten to look up the prisoner who had lied about him. Frustrated at himself, he realized he could easily have carried out his resolution. Why hadn't he thought of the man? He even knew the man's name.

As David climbed into the legal director's car he shared his frustration about not contacting his accuser.

"Be glad that you never did," the legal director said. "The government arranged with him to accuse you. Because he said he had contact with you at the time of the crime, they expected you to make contact with him. They sent spies to follow you the whole time, watching every move you made. Never once did they see you talk to him. You walked by him all the time. You passed by him as you met with hundreds of people, but never once did you look at him nor did he look at you. If you had looked him up or asked him why he lied, you wouldn't be free today."

David's frustration immediately turned to joy. "Praise the Lord!" he exclaimed. "He is able not only to bring promises and memory verses into our heads, but He is able to take thoughts out of our minds too. I had no memory of that man from the moment the gates shut to lock me in prison until they opened to let me out. Only then did I think of that man. What marvelous things God does with our mind when we submit it to Him."

As David rode over the mountains toward home, he could hardly contain his feelings. In his love and gratitude for God, he kept repeating in his mind, *Now to Him who is able to do exceedingly abundantly above all that we ask or think, according to the power that works in us* (Ephesians 3:20, NKJV).

And then he thought of his beloved Becky and the joy of seeing her and the children again. Ten days had seemed like ten years. Perish the horrible thought that had hounded him at every waking moment—fourteen years in prison. Now he'd soon be home!

He looked at the date on his watch, and he remembered something else. Eight years before on this day, he and Becky had pledged to be true to each other for eternity. His heart skipped a beat. His thoughtful, kind God brought him home on their anniversary.

Becky knew nothing about David's release. As she stood looking out the kitchen window while washing dishes, she saw a truck go by. She noticed the official seal on the door, and then she saw it back up and stop in front of their house. Instantly she stiffened with fear. *Could they be coming here to make more problems?* she wondered.

"God, give me courage," she prayed as she dried her hands and started to the door. As she opened the front door she saw a strange man get out of the truck. *Wow! He's so skinny, terribly skinny,* she thought as she watched him walk slowly up the driveway. He seemed to be going in slow motion, taking small steps.

Suddenly she realized who this man was. Rushing out, she screamed, "David!"

He opened his arms, and she fell into them. They clung to each other and cried. Finally David whispered, "Happy anniversary, Sweetie-pie!"

Arm in arm, they walked to the house. The children heard the noise as they entered the living room.

"Daddy, Daddy," they screamed as they ran to him. David knew the joy of being smothered in love, God's love and that of his precious family.

"Come, kids, let's kneel in a circle and thank Jesus for opening the prison doors and bringing Daddy home." Becky gathered them in her arms.

"I knew He would. He heard our prayers. Daddy's home. He's home!" Katrina and Lina chorused over and over. Then they bowed their heads and helped little Carlos fold his hands as David poured out his thanks to their Father in heaven.

Becky and David talked a long while that night after they had tucked the children into bed.

"Sweetie-pie, I learned so much in prison. I'm a changed man. I have finally realized that I own nothing in this world. Everything belongs to God. In that prison cell I had no home, no family to enjoy, no car, no plane. No books to enjoy, no computer. I had nothing but God and the peace He gave when I trusted everything to Him. He alone gave me freedom. He opened the prison doors and allowed me to come back to my precious family. Because of His compassionate love, now I can use all the things He provides that make our life convenient. I owe my life, my health, my breath—everything to Him. He has all of me and everything I have forever."

Becky added her praise.

"As I struggled with depression and fear, I also learned a new trust in Him. When my faith wavered, I called on Him, and peace came. What precious lessons of total commitment God gave us these ten days. I'm so glad we can depend on Him, for He not only hears and answers prayer, but gives us courage when everything seems bleak and hopeless."

The situation in southern Mexico remained tense. Leaders at the South Mexican Union, the Seventh-day Adventist administrative head-quarters, pressed the government to give back the airplane. The military realized that they might lose this valuable airplane, for they had received a court order from the Mexican government to return the airplane. Since they had no intention of complying, they planned another scheme. They decided to have David, an innocent man, thrown back in jail. In order to do this they managed to get an entire village to sign a paper saying that they had seen David using the airplane for illegal purposes, even though he had never landed at that village. Then they sent out a warrant for his arrest.

A Church administrator stopped by the local police headquarters to pick up a legal document, and the desk officer said, "We have a warrant to arrest your *Capitán*. We know he is innocent and suggest you get him out of here fast, for we don't want to see him at all. If we do, we must arrest him again. And this time they won't let him leave prison."

Immediately the conference officials advised David, "*Capitán* Gates, get ready to leave as fast as possible. Pack your belongings, but stay in your home. Tell no one your plans. As soon as you can leave, contact us and we will arrange for you and your family to leave the country. We suggest you leave at night so that your departure will not be known. Later, after you have gone, we'll ship your belongings to you."

With mixed feelings of gratitude and sadness the Gates family left the country they had come to love. They trusted the promise, " 'Have I not commanded you? Be strong and of good courage; do not be afraid, nor be dismayed, for the Lord your God is with you wherever you go' " (Joshua 1:9, NKJV). In faith they committed God's work in southern Mexico to other hands whom God would choose. Eagerly they waited to see where God planned to send them next to serve Him.

CHAPTER 9

Angels by His Side

After a short rest visiting with their parents in the United States, David and Becky received a call from the Inca Union of Seventh-day Adventists to return to Peru. "We need someone to be director of computer services throughout the Union. Please come and work with us in Lima."

For David this assignment meant traveling almost continually. Urgent calls for his expert computer knowledge came without let-up. He'd be one month away from home, one month at the office, then another month out, and then back at the office again. This demanding rat race of service took precious time from his family and communion with God.

Did God have more lessons to teach David about faith and trust? Was David totally depending on Him, and valuing a closer relationship with Him? Had he learned to release his whole life to God?

While driving in Lima one day, David pulled his car from a side road into heavy traffic, five lanes bumper to bumper. He glanced to his left and saw a pistol aimed at his head. He gasped as he looked down the barrel of the gun about one foot away. He expected a shot, and that would be his last moment. He put on his brakes, and so did the cars behind him. The man with the pistol moved on.

Later he found out that he had crossed paths with a gang of bank robbers trying to get away. As they wound through the traffic one man kept his pistol aimed at the other drivers. Every car either slowed down or stopped, and the robbers got away and disappeared in the traffic. David felt God's presence and thanked Him for his angel.

Another afternoon when David was in downtown Lima, he received a message. "A shipment of computers has come into the Port of Callao. Please pick them up."

He had driven his old station wagon to the city even though the starter wasn't working. In Lima it can be difficult to get a new automobile part. The way to fix the problem was to get it rebuilt. He had taken it to an electrician who would rewind the starter. That would take time, and since he had no other vehicle, he had to drive with no starter, relying on others to push him to get the engine going. Knowing the long distance back to the university and the closeness to the Port of Callao, he decided to take a chance. Surely someone would help him get started after he had the computers loaded.

He had no trouble getting to the port. As quickly as he could, he filled out the paperwork, cleared customs, and loaded the station wagon with $70,000 worth of computers. These much-needed machines would be distributed throughout the mission, the university, other schools, and the hospitals. He wondered how many people had sacrificed to give the money for these much-needed computers.

While loading them, he couldn't help but hear the language of the kids around him—foul, obscene, unfit for children or adults. Worried thoughts filled his mind. *If the kids talk like this, what are the morals of the adults? Callao has always been a rough area. And this section of town gets worse as I head up the road toward the university.*

To get the heavily loaded car started, he found three men to push. As he drove out onto the street he reminded God, *You promised that "the angel of the Lord encamps all around those who fear Him, and delivers them."* He added aloud, "Thanks, God, that I'm in a car and moving through this slum area."

Moments later he looked down at the dash as red lights flashed, signaling that the engine had become extremely hot. Then the engine sputtered and froze. He pulled off the street and parked on the gravel. Looking around, he discovered he had parked uphill by an old abandoned bus with no wheels. Probably it had been sitting there for twenty years, a hangout for local drug addicts. He looked at his watch—ten minutes to six and almost sundown.

He quickly took off his tie and suit coat, saying aloud, "God, I'd rather be anyplace else in the world than here. Stay with me." He rushed into a nearby store. The storekeeper looked at him as though he was crazy, wondering what a man like him was doing on the streets at dusk.

"Please give me some water for my car," David said hurriedly.

The man found a bucket and filled it. David poured it into the radiator. He returned with another bucket and poured again. But the radiator wasn't filling up. He looked underneath the car and saw the water pouring out through a hole in the freeze plug. Then he knew he was in deep trouble. He had no way to put water in the car, he didn't have a starter, and all the stores in Lima close promptly at six.

While he stood pondering what to do, he heard a rattle as the storekeeper shut the gates and locked them for the night. He scanned the street, noting that all the shops had closed down. Way down the block he saw a man disappear around the corner. He stood there alone.

He had only one solution. "Please, God, You know I'm in big trouble. I have no way to start this car, and there's $70,000 worth of computers to be used in Your work. I need Your help desperately."

Just then two men came out of the bus. David watched them pick up two big jagged rocks. One man walked around the car one way, and the other one went to the opposite side. David knew how often assaults took place in Lima. Just a few weeks before he had been with a group of friends when several men with a pipe, a chain, and a gun approached them. One threw a rock at him. David saw it in time to dodge as it whizzed behind his head.

Now, standing by the station wagon, he knew that if a jagged rock hit him in the temple, it could do tremendous damage. He understood their intentions. They were waiting to see if he would pull out a weapon.

As they slowly stepped closer David thought, *Lord, You told us to give our life for our friends, but You said nothing about donated computers. These machines aren't worth my family. I don't have to give my life just for computers. Should I leave them? I value Your assets, but I choose not to trade my life for this stuff. If You want to protect Your equipment, You do it. I can't.*

He took one step backward and bumped into another man. *Where did he come from?* David thought. Moments before he had seen no one but the hoodlums with rocks. David felt the man put his hand on his shoulder. Quickly David turned around. The man's face startled him. He had never before seen a face like that, a perfect face, without a flaw. He forgot all about the assault as he stared fascinated at the face that looked at him.

"Your life is in danger. You have to leave."

"I know, you're right," David exclaimed, "but I can't go. My engine is frozen, I don't have a starter, and there's no one to push me."

"I'll push you. Get into your car."

"You can never push me. The station wagon is extremely heavy and filled with equipment. It took three guys to get me started at the pier. Besides, I'm parked on the gravel, and it's uphill. There's no way you can do it. I'm afraid those guys will throw rocks at you."

David glanced at the two men who stood motionless, almost frozen. *Strange,* he thought. *Why aren't they moving? Are they related to Lot's wife?*

The man spoke again. "Get in. I'll push. I know these guys. They're very dangerous. Four of them live in that old bus. They just finished assaulting a whole busload of people. As soon as they got back, they saw you stranded here, and they want your equipment. I came to push your car."

Puzzled at how much he knew, David agreed. "OK, but it won't start." Fearing for the man's life, David watched him go behind the car. But the two men didn't move, just stood holding their rocks. David remembered the standard practice with the pickpockets and thieves in Lima. If anyone intervenes in a robbery and yells, "Watch it, somebody's got your stuff," another person comes up from behind with three razor blades taped between their fingers. They slash up the face of the person trying to help, leaving the skin hanging. This horrible thought filled David's mind. *Will they slash that perfect, beautiful face?*

Even though he knew the man couldn't push, he turned the key. He felt the car move, so he put it in second gear. Still skeptical and pessimistic, David thought, *It can't start. The engine's frozen.* At that moment he let out the clutch and the motor purred as if it were running perfectly.

He put on the brake, and the man yelled, "Get out of here. Hurry up. Please, please!"

David rolled down the window. "It's the custom here in Lima to pay for a favor. I can't leave till I pay you a tip."

"I don't need your tip," the man said firmly. "Go now. Leave, I say."

Stubbornly David insisted, "No, I gotta pay you a tip."

He ran up, and David handed him several *soles.* "Please," the man begged, "get out of here. Go now!"

This time David obeyed and pulled out onto the main road that went down the hill. He traveled about two blocks before the engine sputtered and quit again. He managed to coast into a gas station. As he stopped the car in a lighted area, he began to think about the person who had come to save him.

He put the facts together. The man with the perfect face had appeared out of nowhere; he understood David's trouble and knew the two criminals and their horrible record and what they planned to do. What had kept the two men frozen, holding the rocks? Only supernatural strength, David realized, could enable one man to push the heavy station wagon uphill on gravel. Every detail fit together like a beautiful puzzle.

The words of Psalm 139:5 filled his mind and jolted him. "You hem me in—behind and before; you have laid your hand upon me" (NIV). An angel had actually put his hand on David's shoulder.

Grateful but ashamed of his dullness, David thanked his heavenly Father for sending a mighty angel to care for His slow-to-act child who couldn't seem to catch on even when he had asked for help. What a God!

David did a bit of self-examination as he drove home. *Why do my life situations seem to give my angel problems? I fear I never give my angels any rest. If angels sleep, mine get very little. Could it be because God has chosen to put me on the front lines of service where danger exists? In His love He sends angels to intervene to save my life. I don't try to be difficult, but I seldom hesitate to accept a dangerous mission.*

Could God be telling me to venture out in greater faith? He sent me extra help even though I didn't deserve it. But what kept me from recognizing His divine presence and acting on His suggestions instantly without arguing? Whatever I lack, God, please show me.

Two weeks later David arrived at the Lima bus station after a trip to the North Peruvian Mission. He had installed an accounting system he had written for their computers. Having traveled all night on the bus, he arrived at the station about noon. Lima's bus station is located in the middle of the city in a very dangerous neighborhood. Unfortunately he had to walk three or four blocks through this bad section of town to get to where the taxis waited. Carrying his attaché case, he started out fully aware of a problem. Riding on the bus he hadn't been able to relieve his full bladder for many hours. What to do?

Looking up and down the street, he noticed a small public toilet in a back alley. He knew he'd have to walk through a dangerous, unprotected neighborhood. Since he saw no one, he thought, *I'll just run in and run out and no one will notice.* At the same time he realized that taking a chance like this was like being a bleeding man in a pool of sharks.

He walked quickly up the alley and gave the attendant at the door the usual ten-cent tip. He ran inside, thinking, *I'll only be here fifteen seconds, and be gone fast.*

But someone had noticed him, and he heard a commotion outside. Just as he stood in a very helpless position, a man with a red bandanna around his head and a homemade sword in his hand came running up behind him. David had no way to defend himself. He knew the man wanted his briefcase, his watch, and everything in his pockets.

Just as he came close to David with his sword outstretched, the would-be robber stopped. He had thought David was standing by himself. David also thought he had entered alone. Now he watched the thief look up at something much taller than David. His face turned white and his mouth dropped open. He lowered the sword and held it behind him. Backing up, he stood quietly facing the corner, acting embarrassed.

As soon as David finished, he grabbed his briefcase and walked out. The attendant gaped at him in surprise. He had not expected to see David come out alive. As David hurried down the main street he realized once again that he had experienced the presence of his guardian angel. Though he hadn't seen him, he knew the robber had.

"Thank You, Father," he prayed as he walked, "for the privilege of living in the presence of the One who sends His divine messengers to meet all my needs. Thank You for sending my angel to 'camp around about me and deliver me.' "

As a taxi took him to his home, David kept thinking of all the things that could destroy this relationship with God. *Am I keeping so busy with the mission work that I don't plan significant time each day to study God's Word and pray? Do I use my spare minutes reading magazines, newspapers, or books, or looking at TV or videos, things that could take away my taste for spiritual things? Am I allowing friends to draw me away from Jesus? Are my choices of food and drink those that will keep my mind clear so that I'm alert to Satan's endeavors to assault me spiritually? Am I enjoying that precious relationship that always encloses me in God's loving arms?* He prayed out loud, "Help me to give glory to You in all I do."

Too Much Stress

In 1990 the Inca Union church administration in Peru named David as a delegate to the Indianapolis General Conference business session. They needed a man skilled in translating from English to Spanish. Though David's language abilities enabled him to converse in Portuguese, German, and French, he could give accurate, rapid translations into Spanish, word for word. Spanish delegates on the floor appreciated his services as he translated the sermons and business sessions into their headphones. This kept him busy from early morning till late at night. He spent eight weeks in the United States working continually under stressful conditions.

When he returned home to Lima he experienced weariness that he couldn't shake. His raw nerves, his negative mental attitude, his lack of ability to cope, seemed so unlike the usual upbeat David. Something was wrong. He appeared to be a changed man. His pessimistic outlook puzzled Becky and the children. They found him hard to live with for the next three months. He seemed to hate everything. He hated being at home. He hated being at work. He put everybody through a difficult time.

Becky suspected that his overwork had caused burnout and that he might be on the verge of a breakdown. She prayed for insight to understand her troubled husband and asked God for solutions.

Something that shook up both of them was the sudden break-up of the marriage of their closest friends, another missionary couple, who chose to divorce.

David became very sensitive and protective of Becky. He feared the Peruvian students had the idea that American wives were easy prey. One day he heard a student call Becky by her first name. Never in a formal Spanish society do students address faculty members by their first name. It is not appropriate unless the people involved have become close friends. David's stressed, confused mind began to suspect this young student. Was he trying to lure Becky away?

Becky had been helping the theology student by typing his final research paper. One evening when the student came by, David again heard him address her as Becky. This angered David. How could a student violate the custom by addressing a faculty member this way?

Again the thought came to him, could this student be trying to take advantage of his wife? He forgot his usual practice of praying in every situation. Instead of looking for a solution, David made life difficult for Becky. "Throw him out of the house. You better tell him not to do that anymore," he threatened.

Becky felt that David, as her husband, should speak to the student and say, "You must never do that again. If you do that, you don't come back again." When she explained her feelings to David, he responded in anger, "You must never allow that student to use your first name!"

Never before had he spoken to her like that. She understood that his stressful condition was blinding him to his unreasonable demands. More and more he reacted to her with impatience. Even an ideal marriage like theirs faced jeopardy.

Fearing that David could be close to a complete breakdown, Becky prayed that God would impress him to accept a suggestion from her. "David, we haven't had a vacation for a long time. We must get away. Can you please arrange for a quiet place where we can go to be alone and rest a while."

Her plan worked.

"I do need to make a business trip to do the accounting closure for one of our small hospitals near the Brazil border. After I finish my work we could stay in one of the rustic cabins along the Amazon River. I'm sure they'd rent a canoe to us. And that's on our tenth wedding anniversary. Would you like that?"

"Oh, yes! I'd love to just be with you anywhere, even in the middle of the Amazon River."

They arranged for a reliable young woman to take care of the children, and the two of them went on a much-needed second honeymoon.

"David, this is great," Becky giggled as they paddled the dugout canoe. "To think that I'm privileged to be with my Tall, Dark, and Handsome on this mighty river. Must be three or four miles wide here. Coming from dry, brown Lima, the green jungle and the colorful birds remind me of heaven."

"You amaze me, Sweetie-pie. Obviously you are not the normal sophisticated, candlelight, romantic girl. Not many girls love getting in a canoe in the jungle, paddling across the river, and declaring it the most romantic thing they can think of. How come you have so much fun living where there's no refrigerator, no electricity, no running water, and you can go around barefoot?"

"That's where we met, David, when we were kids. Doing those kinds of things together bonded our friendship. What precious memories! But I do appreciate the civilized surprises too. I'm glad you keep me supplied with perfume and bring me roses and other flowers. You're so thoughtful, inventing special little surprises for my birthday and anniversaries."

"But one time I did forget. That was the year we moved from Mexico to Peru."

"You felt terrible when you realized the day slipped by without a word from you. But a couple days later you came home early and acted so strange. You kept looking out the window, gazing down the street, walking around and looking again."

David smiled. "And when you asked, 'What's going on?' I said, 'Oh, nothing.' "

"Yes, and a few minutes later I saw a big truck stop in front of our house. And then those men unloaded a piano. What a thrill! You more than made up for forgetting my birthday."

"God has given us so much joy together," David said reflectively. "Remember that Sabbath day shortly before we got married when we sat together in a hammock and made a covenant with God. 'We'll go wherever You send us. Just keep us true to You. If it is Your will, please keep us together, standing hand in hand, waiting for Jesus to come in the clouds.' "

"Yes, David, and God has given me peace. Wherever He has led us, He's made our home a little heaven. We can trust Him to keep us until He comes."

During this short vacation on the Amazon, David snapped back to his old self. Only then did he realize he had experienced severe burnout. With his arm around Becky, he prayed, "God, please alert me to my weakness. Forgive me for allowing myself to overwork. Keep me close to You so I'll never get caught in that miserable place again."

After almost five years of constant traveling, Becky and David decided he could no longer endure a routine that demanded such long hours away from home. Their family had grown. They had adopted two more children—Katia, a lovely Peruvian girl, five years older than their daughter, Lina, and little Kristopher, also a Peruvian, four years younger than Carlos.

In 1992 David asked for an appointment to meet with the Inca Union church leaders.

"I have greatly enjoyed the privilege of working with you," he told them. "I love my work, but I'm sure I need a change. We now have a family of five. These children need a father at home, especially the two youngest, both boys. We must not sacrifice our children's spirituality to the demands of my job. I need a change. Maybe I could teach at the university. I'll be glad to do whatever God asks, but I must have more time to be home with my family."

"We're sorry, but at present we must cut back on personnel. Out of ninety overseas salaries assigned to our division, we're forced to cut back to twenty-two. No salary budgets are available elsewhere. We need your skills and expertise on the job you have now. Computer specialists are hard to come by."

"I understand your problem," David assured them. "However, after much prayer, we feel that God has impressed us that I cannot continue in this stressful work even though I've enjoyed doing it for five years. Our children hardly see their daddy. They need both parents. I believe the next best thing for us to do is ask for a permanent return to the

United States. I feel a need to complete graduate training in computer software engineering."

After they had made the decision, David and Becky felt relieved and challenged. That night they talked for several hours after the children had gone to bed.

"I'm sure God has special plans for our family's future. I know He will give us a vision to see by faith what others see only by sight. I'm confident that under His guidance and leadership we will see His power and leading. Our part is to focus on His will and not what people tell us. Are you willing to learn to rely exclusively on His divine omnipotence?"

Becky laid her head on David's shoulder. "I'm willing to go anywhere God sends us. I believe He'll give us a vision of service that will enable us to see infinite possibilities instead of numerous problems. Won't it be exciting to see Him open up opportunities and take care of the obstacles? I can hardly wait to find out what God plans for us."

CHAPTER 11

Under New Management

As David was completing his graduate studies in software engineering in 1993, he was contacted by Dr. Sylvan Lashley, president of Caribbean Union College in Port-of-Spain, Trinidad.

"We need you desperately as director of computer services, but we have a problem," the president said. "We have no overseas budget for you."

"Can you find someone else who can do the job?" David asked.

"We have no one who has the training and expertise you have."

"Could I come as an AVS [Adventist Volunteer Service] worker? Would you provide a home for a family of seven, and a stipend so we can eat? If so, we'll be glad to accept your invitation. We work for God, not for money. We know God will provide as we move forward."

And God came through again. After three months on the job, an overseas budget suddenly became available and the college assigned it to him. So David began teaching part time at Caribbean Union College in Trinidad and also working as director of computer services for the territory of the Caribbean Union Conference of Seventh-day Adventists. He often took his computer students on trips to help him install software in various countries throughout the Union.

Sometimes his duties meant a flight to Georgetown, Guyana. As he accompanied the Guyana conference administration for a visit to the jungle interior, David became aware of the great needs of the Amerindians, especially the Akawayo and Arecuna tribes that live around Mount Roraima. This section of southwest Guyana is a long way from anywhere, surrounded by vast jungles and treacherous rivers, steep mountains, and numerous waterfalls. Here the borders of three countries meet—Venezuela, Brazil, and Guyana.

At this place David discovered the Davis Indians. These people, descendants of old Chief Owkwa, who in vision had talked with an angel many times, seemed nobler than other Indians did. Because of the angel's instruction the chief had taught them many Bible truths, which the Davis Indians still followed. In 1911 the courageous missionary O. E. Davis had fulfilled the angel's promise to Chief Owkwa of the white man who would come with the Black Book to teach them more about God and heaven. Even though he lived only a short time, they loved Davis and accepted his teachings.

Unlike many of the other Indian tribes David had worked with in other countries, the Davis Indians did not beg, but they did give. They gave to others generously of what they had.

David learned that a missionary had never lived in the village of Kaikan. When he returned home, he said to Becky and the children, "I wonder how many of these dear Indians die from lack of medical and spiritual help. What a great blessing an airplane could be in reaching many of those inaccessible villages."

"Oh, Sweetie-pie," Becky exclaimed, "I want to go there so badly. We could help those dear people so much!"

After several years of service at Caribbean Union College, David found these lines written by an unknown author:

> O pray not for easy lives, pray to be strong! Pray not for tasks equal to your powers, pray for powers equal to your tasks; then the doing of your work shall be no miracle, but you shall be a miracle to the praise of Him who has made you who you are.

"Becky, please read this and then let's talk. I have an idea." David's intense manner alerted Becky that he had something special to share.

"We've been working overseas for nearly sixteen years. We began as volunteers. Later we managed on a national salary for nearly four years. Now we've been blessed with a comfortable overseas salary and benefits. God has blessed us with five children who will soon need academy and college education. They are our first responsibility."

He paused. Becky's heart began to beat faster as she waited for him to continue. "God has given me a burden to become a missionary among the Davis Indians in the interior of Guyana at the village of Kaikan. The Guyana conference has no budget for that area. I feel impressed by the Holy Spirit that we should become volunteers again. But how can we manage with our five children?"

"Are you suggesting that we take our large family into the interior with no means of survival in a jungle village just as my parents did in Peru and later in Africa? My sisters and their families followed their example. We could too."

"We've already decided to go home to the States next year. Why don't we postpone our return trip to the U.S. for one year and experiment with God? I believe this is the time to give our lives totally in commitment to Him. Let's talk this over with our children. God can supply all our needs two hundred miles back into the jungle. Are we willing to take this risk and depend totally on Him? We'll not tell anyone of our needs and see what God can do. We'll soon know if God is telling the truth. Isn't it time we find out for ourselves?"

"I'm willing, Sweetie-pie. Our God who controls the universe can surely take care of a family of seven. Our kids need to know if God is for real firsthand, before they leave home and go to college," added Becky. "They will learn to live simply, like you and I did as children. Like us they'll find true happiness in service."

David talked with his boss, the Union president. "We have definitely decided to go back to the States. But first, we'd like permission to go to Guyana for a year on a volunteer basis and establish God's message with the Davis Indians in the village of Kaikan."

"Why don't you stay here for another year? I have no idea where we can get a competent computer science teacher," the president said.

"I'm sure God will supply your need for a teacher. We could return directly to the U.S., but we'd rather give our volunteer services to Guyana for that year."

Reluctantly the president consented. "It's a good work. They need it. We're willing to release you."

That evening at supper David broke the good news to the children. "Sounds great, Daddy, like real adventure." Katrina was always looking for something new.

One of the girls added skeptically, "No electricity? No running water? No bathrooms? Can we live like that?"

Ignoring her, the others chimed in, "When do we start packing, Daddy?"

"The sooner the better. I'll make arrangements to fly across to Georgetown. Since no roads lead to Kaikan, we'll need to catch a ride with a bush pilot to go into the interior."

David shared his dream with his relatives in the States through email. "We plan to establish a volunteer medical mission post among the Davis Indians," he wrote. Becky's sister, Betsy, and brother-in-law, Ted Burgdorff, who lived in Chowchilla, California, decided to join them for a short time.

The day that he received his last paycheck, David's emotions hit the panic button. Was he jumping off a cliff? Was this presumption or faith? No more money coming in. He prayed, "God, please give me assurance, peace, and trust." Instantly, Jeremiah 33:3 flashed into his mind. "Call unto me, and I will answer thee, and shew thee great and mighty things, which thou knowest not" (KJV).

He did keep all their airline tickets for a flight home, should they discover this wasn't God plan for them. "This is a test for You, God," he said aloud. "If You can't feed us and handle our finances, we'll have to go home. But in my heart I think we'll use these tickets only for a short visit home sometime."

The people of Kaikan heard that a missionary family might come, but they didn't believe the good news. However, when the Gates family arrived in Georgetown, they called the village on the short-wave radio. "We're coming! Another family with their three daughters will come too."

After the family landed in Kaikan, the greeting they received almost overwhelmed them. The people of the village had arranged little posts from the runway all the way to the church, with jungle flowers on each post. Above the church door they had placed a large sign that read, "WELCOME TO KAIKAN." The entire village of 150 people waited at the airstrip to meet them. A choir sang as the Gates family walked to the church.

"I feel like King David coming to Jerusalem with the ark of the covenant," David whispered to Becky. "They couldn't treat the president of the country any better. These people really want a missionary. How blessed we are! I've heard of missionaries who have been killed or had rocks thrown at them by the people they came to serve. This is truly red carpet treatment." Becky and David began to cry as they and their children and relatives were led to specially prepared seats. For two hours they listened to a well-planned concert.

SDA church near runway at Kaikan

Then the villagers took the family to a small house near the river, similar to their own homes. Smiling, one of the villagers said, "We've made it ready for you. We hope you like it."

Knowing that jungle people often crowd several families into one house, they squeezed in. The adults smiled as they looked around at the cramped quarters, but the kids thought it great fun to hunker down on the floor together. The small cupboard contained no food, so they went to bed a little hungry.

The next day the village people realized that their missionaries had little to eat for breakfast. From every direction people began to come loaded with packs on their backs full of bananas, papayas, root vegetables—every kind of food they had.

Typical of those who brought food to the house was Claude Anselmo, who immediately offered his services. Speaking good English, he said, "I was a policeman in Georgetown, but because of problems in my home, I've returned to my real home, Kaikan. I'd be glad to help you get settled and fit into village life. If there's anything I can do, please tell me."

Claude soon became David's right-hand man, caring for many details that would have been neglected without him.

The adult missionaries, being nurses, immediately noticed the medical needs of the people. Even though the government maintained a small dispensary in the village, the community health worker had only a few months' training and lacked many medications. "We must begin to make plans to assist the health worker in providing the villagers with health services," they concluded.

A beautiful river with pure, clean water ran by their little home. This served for cooking, bathing, and washing clothes. A nearby spring provided good drinking water, though they still took the precaution of adding bleach. A convenient outhouse provided toilet facilities. At first they cooked just like the villagers, chopping their wood and using a campfire-like stove outdoors. They soon realized that the women were spending a lot of time on this primitive method, so David procured a propane gas stove that speeded up the cooking and gave more time to serve the villagers. Solar panels charged up their twelve-volt battery that ran the high-frequency radio and lights at night. An inverter provided electricity to operate their notebook computer and Becky's sewing machine. The children had a vast playground—the jungle and river around them.

After they had been in Kaikan a few months, Becky told David, "I love this place. My joy comes from seeing our children value this important fact—they've discovered that happiness doesn't come from things, but in serving the Lord. They radiate joy and contentment living this simple lifestyle.

"Being mother and teacher, scrubbing clothes on a board by the river, navigating on the aluminum boat we use to cross the river to the little store—all this provides laughter and fun as we work together."

Both the missionaries and village folk realized the need to build a larger home. With Claude leading out, the people from neighboring villages joined with the Kaikan villagers to cut down trees, prepare the lumber with their chain saws and help with the construction. The ground floor of the two-story house consisted of a large kitchen and dining area, plus a room to be used as a clinic to see patients. The upstairs had a spacious living room with a large glassless corner window, and four bedrooms. The men rigged up an outside shower enclosure especially for Becky.

David's brother-in-law, Ted, built the beds, cupboards, closets, and benches and a table. He also set up barrels to catch rainwater and piped it right into the kitchen sink.

All of the Gates and Burgdorff children contributed to the project. They helped in Sabbath School, leading out wherever they were needed in church activities. The older girls used their musical talents to organize a junior choir. The village kids loved to sing.

House built for Gates family in Kaikan. L to R: Jay Lantry, Carlos, Kris, Becky.

During that first year one of the teachers at the Kaikan elementary school had to leave before the school year ended. The village people came to David and Becky's daughter Lina and her cousin Heidi, both fourteen. "Would you teach for us?" they asked. Lina and her cousin accepted the challenge. Each day they dedicated the precious students to God, asking for wisdom. He blessed their efforts. When the school year ended, the head mistress told Becky,

"Kaikan's elementary school came in first place on the examinations, all because of the excellent teaching of your girls." Later, second daughter Katrina, her cousin Kristen, and their friend Sarah Eirich also helped teach school.

"We must teach the village folk practical ways to take care of their bodies," Becky suggested to her sister, Betsy.

"Yes, they have no knowledge of health principles and disease prevention. Let's plan for classes lasting six months. We'll team-teach. Since Ted's also a nurse, he can join us."

The classes proved to be successful. Other villages nearby heard of the First Aid course the missionaries were offering. They walked a long way each Sunday for many weeks to receive this training.

In addition, Betsy taught music classes and started a Pathfinder club. ADRA provided some treadle sewing machines that Becky used to teach the village women how to sew. Besides their own clothing, the women learned to sew uniforms for the Pathfinders.

"It's so exciting to see the joy in the eyes of these dear people as their lives become more meaningful with these new skills!" Becky exclaimed to David one day.

A few months later, David's parents came to help. David's father immediately began preparing the soil and planting a garden. His mother's years of medical experience enabled her to help in the clinic.

One Sabbath after David's father had preached, Claude Anselmo met him outside, "If you had made a call today, I would have given my life to God." The Gates family had been praying for this moment, and they rejoiced greatly as they watched David's father baptize Claude in the river a few days later. From that day Claude was a powerful influence for good in the village. He was also highly respected by the armed forces and the govern-

Baptism at Kaikan with Pastor Bacchus.

ment. Whenever the Gateses left Kaikan, he cared for their home and managed many details in the village.

As word spread of the missionaries' presence, people from other villages came with requests. "Could you come to our village and teach us too?"

"Where do you live?" David asked.

"Not very far away. Just four days walking that way," they said, pointing over the jungle-covered mountains. David couldn't imagine walking, climbing, and crossing rivers for four days, staying one day, and walking back for four days. Eight days without accomplishing anything!

This was just the sort of need David and Becky had envisioned before moving to Guyana. Without roads or navigable rivers, an aviation program was almost indispensable. They had dreamed about and prayed for an airplane, and as a result God had nudged them to go forward in faith, to dream bigger visions.

CHAPTER 12

GAMAS Is Born

"Becky, there's only one solution—an airplane," her pilot husband spoke with conviction. "But right now, we will barely have enough money to buy medicines and food."

Becky and David prayed for God's guidance. Should they step out in faith?

"God will open the way," David concluded. "First, I must contact the government and lay the groundwork for an aviation program."

From the beginning, officials resisted his appeals. But he ignored their No's and asked, "What form do I fill out?"

"This form." And they handed him a piece of paper. He quickly filled it out.

"What test do I have to take?" He took the test. He did everything they required and ended up with a Guyana commercial pilot's license, even though it took almost a year and no one seemed to want him to have one.

"Well, Becky," he reported, "I've laid the ground work. But we have no money to begin an aviation mission service in Guyana. Still the promise rings in my ears, 'He who calls you is faithful, who also will do it.' "

"We've relied on that promise many times before. We can't wear it out from overuse," Becky said, smiling at David. "I'm impressed that before we settle in Guyana you should go to the States to buy an airplane. We have $5,000 in savings in the U.S. You know, the money that the General Conference gave us to move all our things from Trinidad and Tobago back to the States. Let's send only a few things back and use the rest toward the purchase of an airplane, even though we had planned to leave that money in the bank for an emergency."

"You're right, Sweetie-pie. As I hear of the many sick in the villages dying because there's no way to transport them to a hospital, I feel this is the emergency. Even though $5,000 can't come close to buying an airplane, I know God will multiply it. Yes, I'll go."

She hugged him close. "You and God have such a fantastic relationship. I know He loves to answer your prayers."

Going forward on God's promises, David headed home to the United States. Upon arriving at his parents' home, David bought a copy of a magazine called *Trade-A-Plane,* which listed thousands of airplanes for sale. He studied it carefully, scanning each ad for his dream of the ideal airplane for the jungles.

"What are you looking for, David?" his father asked.

"I'm looking for an airplane to buy."

"With only $5,000! You know you can't buy an airplane with that."

"That's not my problem, Daddy. First, I must find the airplane. Then God is responsible to provide the money. I think I found just what I wanted. I'm going to call the owner now."

David explained what he needed and why. The man answered, "If you come and look at it, and you think it will serve well for mission service, I'll drop the price several thousand dollars and sell it to you."

When David hung up the phone, he announced. "I'm going to go see that airplane."

"With what money are you going to buy it?" his father asked again.

"Daddy, that's not my problem. My job is to find the right airplane first before I expect God to give me the money. When I need it, God will keep His promise, 'My God shall supply all your need according to His riches in glory by Christ Jesus.' "

His father's face still had a questioning look.

"OK, Daddy. Maybe I should explain. I know this is the not usual way to do business. The normally accepted policy is to have the money up front before an airplane is purchased. Also, the pilot has one main job, to operate the plane. He does not take on other responsibilities."

"So how do you plan to operate?" his father wondered.

"We have chosen to live totally by faith, trusting that God knows how to provide for our financial needs. He knows our needs better than we do. Now I'm not against others operating their businesses with a sound operational budget before they proceed. But since we chose to be volunteers, we have no monthly paycheck on which to make a budget. We've decided God knows a lot more about finances than we do. He's capable of directing His work. He loves to care for His children. Already He's done a great job. We've read about what God did for George Mueller, Hudson Taylor, and others, and we are confident He will do the same for us. So we base our decisions on His promises. We intend to press forward by faith to see what new area God will open up."

"I understand, Son. Mother and I agree that we must be absolutely committed to God in faith and risk all for Him too."

David's brother-in-law, Bill Norton, was sitting nearby, listening to the conversation. David asked him, "Would you like to go with me to check out that airplane? It's a long haul from California to North Carolina. I'd like your company."

"Yes, sure, I'd love to," he replied.

The day they left for North Carolina, the parents of David's brother-in-law, Ted, told David, "We have some savings in the bank. We'd be willing to make you a loan, interest free, to buy this airplane. You can pay us back as God gives you the money."

So David left with money in his pocket. He bought the airplane. "This plane needs a lot of repairs," he concluded. "Though it needs almost everything done over again, the price is right. I can see it has great possibilities. I'll fly it to Kentucky. We'll need to rebuild the engine there. After it is completely overhauled, we'll give it a new paint job, do some sheet metal work, and install the radios." While the plane was being worked on in Kentucky, David took his family and the Burgdorffs into the village of Kaikan and returned to the U.S. to assist with the plane maintenance.

After some time, David found himself installing the rebuilt engine on the plane. The cold December winds chilled the unheated hangar as David labored to finish the engine installation. Desperately lonely from his months away from home, and uncomfortable from the cold, David felt a great depression settle over him. All evening he struggled against the darkness while painfully connecting cables and tightening nuts.

This is not normal for me, thought David to himself. *I feel like rolling up into a fetal position and hiding under a blanket.* Remembering his Mighty Refuge, he took his case to the Lord. *Dear Jesus,* he groaned inwardly. *If this great darkness is somehow caused by the enemy, please take it from me.* Sixty seconds later he found himself whistling and full of normal enthusiasm. After having experienced the darkness of depression, David realized that his optimism and joy are daily gifts from the Lord.

The next morning, still bubbling over with joy, David suddenly had an idea. Why not surprise his family and spend Christmas with them in Kaikan? Yes, it would take some financial sacrifice, but family was definitely worth it. A few quick phone calls and it was all arranged. He had reserved the last seat on the weekly charter flight into Kaikan. He told no one of his arrival.

Becky ran up to the runway to meet the flight and send out some mail for David. On their second Christmas apart in twenty years, she would miss him terribly. As the plane landed and taxied up, one of the Amerindian women asked Becky, "Isn't that Elder Gates sitting in the plane?" Her heart skipped a beat, but Becky quickly responded, "Oh, it can't be. He won't be home for Christmas this year. He is still in the U.S. working on the plane." A tear rolled down her cheek as she peered hopefully toward the plane.

As her Tall, Dark, and Handsome stepped out, she ran to him and threw herself into his arms. She walked hand in hand with him down to the house to share the surprise with the kids.

A month later, David returned to the U.S. to pick up the plane in Kentucky and fly it to Andrews University in Berrien Springs, Michigan. There the director of maintenance for Andrews Airpark, Brooks Payne, worked with aviation maintenance students to complete final preparations for the plane's departure. Brooks felt especially thrilled to be part of this mission endeavor and dedicated long hours of overtime to ensuring that the work done was top notch. David's dedication instilled in them a desire for mission aviation as they put in new interior upholstery, new brakes, new wheels, new instrument panel, new cables, and fixed the corrosion. They also worked on the high-frequency radio.

A man who had heard of David's project dropped by the hangar. David explained to him, "Highly modified, this two-seater Cessna 150 will be ideal for jungle airstrip operations." The plane had a Short Take-off and Landing (STOL) kit and wing-tip alterations that would increase the lift. Large balloon tires would enable it to land on many kinds of terrain.

"May I help with this project?" the man asked as he pulled out his checkbook. Funds started coming in from many other sources. Three months after the purchase of the plane the loan to Ted's family had been completely paid off. David exclaimed, "God did it again! We moved forward in faith, and the waters parted!" The Guyana Adventist Medical Aviation Service would soon be a reality.

Finally the renovations were completed. David smiled as he inspected the beautiful white plane with yellow and red stripes, black registration numbers, and green lettering (the colors of the Guyanese flag). "You've done a great job, guys," he told the students. "The new high-powered engine and high-lift wing will make this an ideal aircraft to begin medical evacuation operations."

"Do you have everything arranged with the Guyanese officials?" the crew at Andrews asked.

"No. Future progress is in God's hands. We'll face great odds in establishing an aviation project in Guyana. The secular government doesn't appear favorable to a missionary airplane in the interior. They do not as yet see what an asset the church can be to help raise the quality of life in the jungle. So far their response has been, 'No, no, no.' I'm trusting God to do great things."

"Tell us your plan of operation after God works out the problems." The students showed deep interest.

"We have three objectives. First, free medical evacuation services. We will respond to any medical emergency and take the patient to the nearest hospital. Second, we'll offer health education. Very few know the basic principles of healthful living. Third, we believe a key factor in our success is communication. Every village with a runway has a radio, so the patients know when we'll arrive."

"What type of runways do you use for landing?"

"The length varies from 900 feet to 1,500 feet. All require the steady touch of a veteran bush pilot. Some are dangerous when wet. Others have wind conditions that are safe in the morning, but difficult in the evening."

"Wow, you face lots of challenges. We're glad you and God are in this together. We've worked too hard to have this plane crash."

"Thanks so much, fellas. I need your prayers for wisdom and safety. The time has come for me to fly this plane to Guyana. I'll allow two days to fill out the logbook entries and complete the FAA paperwork. Leif Aaen [a recent graduate from Andrews Aviation Maintenance School] will be my copilot during the trip. He plans to stay as a volunteer. I'll stop to spend the weekend with my family in Illinois, and then we'll be on our way to South America."

CHAPTER 13

From Miami to Kaikan

Family, neighbors, and friends gathered around the plane on the grass strip of the Gates family's Illinois farm. David's father, his voice usually strong, quivered as he prayed, "Thank You, God, for providing this mission plane. Send Your angels to care for David and Leif during the many hours of flying to South America. We dedicate them and this plane to the work of God in Guyana."

Taxiing to the end of the grass runway, David and Leif took off at about 6:00 P.M. At the first fuel stop in Chattanooga at 10:30 P.M. they filled not only their wing tanks, but also their fifteen-gallon ferry tank. Beautiful weather made the long, all-night flight to Orlando, Florida, a joy. They touched down at 5:00 A.M., slept for five hours in the darkened pilot's lounge, and then headed for Opa Locka International Airport in Miami. Business in Miami kept them all Monday afternoon.

Early Tuesday they refilled the plane with fuel. Because of a blackout, the offices were dark, so David filed his flight plan and paid for the fuel in very dim light. By 7:00 A.M. they were airborne en route to Stella Maris, a small island in the Bahamas.

As they flew over Nassau, a voice from air traffic control spoke over the radio. "You left your passports in Miami." Immediately David checked his fanny pack and found them. He was confused by the message. What could be missing?

As they refueled in Stella Maris, Leif loaned David the money for payment so he wouldn't have to dig through the cargo for his briefcase. Later in the night, after landing on the island of Grand Turk, David pulled out the luggage to look for the briefcase that contained his money. Panic hit as he exclaimed, "Leif, I left my cash bag in that darkened office with two thousand dollars in it! Most places where we'll refuel won't accept a credit card for fuel purchases."

David felt sick in his stomach as he took off for Puerto Rico. He talked to God a lot during that lonely five-hour night flight. "Heavenly Father, You hold control of this whole project in spite of my human bungles and deficiencies. If I left my cash in Miami, You'll see us through this problem. You know if it's been found and the cash is still in place. I'm resting myself in Your hands."

Again assurance came to him through God's Word. "Then they cried unto the Lord in their trouble, and he saved them out of their distresses" (Psalm 107:13, KJV).

As soon as David got out of the plane at San Juan International Airport, he headed for a pay phone. He knew that the Miami Aviation Corporation stayed open twenty-four hours a day. To his questions the man on duty answered, "Yes, the manager left this note. It says, 'Found David's bag on the counter where he paid for the fuel. I opened it, saw the cash, and immediately stuck it in the safe. Tell Gates to call in the morning to make arrangements to get it.' "

Filled with gratitude and praise for a heavenly Father who continues to care for His imperfect children, David slept well that night.

The next morning David spoke to the manager in Miami. She told him that she would convert the money into money orders. "I will send the whole bag to Puerto Rico immediately," she said, and added, "We'll deal with this matter at no charge to you. We treat all of our customers in the same way."

Though he lost a day's travel waiting for the package to arrive, David rejoiced at God's blessings and took advantage of the time, picking up supplies and stocking up on food for the trip. He knew he had some long flights ahead to reach Guyana by Friday.

The parcel-post plane was delayed and didn't arrive until 11:00 A.M. Thursday, so David and Leif didn't get off the ground until 12:30 P.M., headed for Martinique. A large ash cloud from the recent eruption of the volcano on Montserrat caused them to change their flight plan to a five-hour flight ending with a beautiful sunset in Fort-de-France. Here David had to refuel, get a weather briefing, and file his instrument flight plan, speaking French with a Spanish accent.

The next island stop, St. Lucia, had two high volcanic mountains. Adrenaline shot through David's nervous system as he flew at nearly three thousand feet above the peaks. The plane was tossed up and down by turbulent wind drafts from the volcanoes. "Thank You, God, for Your powerful angels that fly along with us," he prayed in gratitude.

Later, comforting specks of light appeared out of the darkness along the coast of St. Vincent. Finally David saw a glow from Grenada through fog and low-lying clouds. He got excited as the coastline of Trinidad began to show on the horizon.

"I lived here for three years and taught flying at this airport," David told Leif. "Below is Maracas Valley, where I taught at Caribbean Union College." They landed at 9:30 P.M. While waiting to clear customs and immigration, he called his old boss and friend, Roland Thomson, the Union treasurer, who immediately came to see the plane and help him refuel it. He invited the two pilots to spend the few remaining hours of the night at his home.

They lifted off at 6:30 A.M. and touched down at Guyana three and a half hours later. Just before they landed at the small airport in downtown Georgetown, David explained to Leif, "Permission for us to fly on to Kaikan will take a miracle from God. Usually this takes weeks or even months after the plane's arrival. I so much want to be there for my daughter Katrina's eighth-grade graduation. And my niece Kristen will be graduating as well. Let's pray."

After David landed in Georgetown, several aircraft mechanics and pilots watched him taxi in. The airport administrator ordered, "Go park your airplane in that back corner way over there. You won't be flying that plane for a long, long time."

"You may be right, but I really don't believe that's the case," David told him. "I believe I'm going to fly that plane out right away. May I park it here while I talk to the director of civil aviation?"

"Why?"

"I want to fly into the interior today." All of the men laughed.

"We've never heard of such a thing. Even when we bring airplanes into the country we have to wait two or three months. You certainly won't be flying anywhere today!"

On the way to the office of civil aviation, David claimed God's promise, "Through God we shall do valiantly" (Psalm 108:13, KJV). Inside the office, he made his request to the assistant director.

"I really cannot let you fly," the assistant director responded. "You need more experience."

"I've been flying for ten years in the jungle."

"No, no. I mean you need more experience in Guyana."

"I've already landed in the village of Kaikan at least ten times in both Islanders and Cessna 206s, as a copilot with air taxi pilots. I am very familiar with both the route and the airfield itself. Why would I need more than ten trips?"

"You need twenty at least before you are used to it."

"I fear that after I've flown twenty, you'll say I need forty. Please, may I talk to the director himself?"

"Well, you're in luck. The director is in today, but he won't let you fly either."

"May I still see him, please?"

David walked to the director's office, praying as he went. The director's first words sounded the same. "No, I'm sorry, but I can't let you fly there. You need more experience. I must deny your request because the flight is too dangerous. You need at least twenty trips."

Feeling a little discouraged, David shot another prayer to God for guidance and pleaded, "Don't get angry with me, but I have one more argument in my favor. You see, my family lives in Kaikan, and my daughter and my niece graduate from the eighth grade on Monday. I've been in the States for some time. Please, I'd be so happy to see my family and attend the graduation."

"You mean your family doesn't live here in Georgetown?"

"No, my family lives in Kaikan. That's our home village. The runway is near my home. I know it very well."

David, Joe Alexander, and Claude Anselmo working on the Cessna 150

"Oh, that changes everything. I had no idea your family lived there. Your confidence is evident and contagious. You have my permission to make the flight. Please be careful. Here, let me sign the form. You may leave today." David walked out with the permission form in his hand and a prayer of praise in his heart.

The mouth of the airport administrator dropped open when David asked, "Please have this plane refueled while I file my flight plan." He handed the air traffic controller his permission form signed by the director of civil aviation. No one could believe he would be allowed to take off for the interior the same day he arrived in Guyana. But David knew that only God could change attitudes. As his plane lifted off, his voice shouted heavenward, "For with God nothing shall be impossible."

David flew for two hours over the jungle, recognizing landmarks along the way. When he began the descent into Kaikan, his eyes filled with tears. As they taxied in, he saw the whole village waiting. Before he had even unbuckled his seat belt and stepped out of the plane, most of the men of the village had already stepped up, all trying to hug him at once. The villagers formed a circle around the airplane for a special thanksgiving service to the God who made all these things possible.

David's voice broke several times as he poured out his gratefulness and joy to God that the medical plane had finally landed at home in Kaikan. The jungle resounded with praises to the wonderful God these Indians served. Becky imagined she heard the angels singing, too, at this precious homecoming.

Just twenty minutes before Sabbath they pushed the plane into its tie-down position next to the mango trees.

CHAPTER 14

Davis Indian Industrial College

David's buying an airplane proved that God still loves to work miracles. But what about operating the plane? Fuel is extremely expensive in Guyana, especially in the interior. But in faith the Guyana Adventist Medical Aviation Service (GAMAS) began transporting medical patients to the hospitals and back again.

Each time David spent money for food, medicine, or fuel, someone would fly in and leave a gift, saying, "I feel impressed to give this to you for your expenses."

This procedure of giving and receiving even more began to sink into David's head. *Giving is actually receiving!* That is, when God is your Financier.

One time a large amount of money came in. "Are we doing something wrong?" he asked Becky. "We must not be spending enough toward the needs here. Could God be telling us He wants us to think and act bigger, to do more for these people?"

"Looks that way to me. I've noticed that the teenagers need a school beyond primary (grades 1-5) and secondary (grades 6-8). I see a lack in this area for a school to prepare the youth for service. They stand around idle. Some get into trouble." Becky swung her arm in a circle. "Too many of our youth in these villages are drifting away from God's church."

"Right! They need a boarding academy. Let's build one." David's enthusiasm was growing. "Until 1963 missionaries operated a thriving school near Paruima. When a new government took over, everything shut down. The

Toll family, forced to evacuate, closed the school in 1964. We need to check out that site. It's less than a mile from the village. I understand the ground is extremely fertile there. Anything grows."

Always a man of action, David arranged to fly to the Paruima airstrip, which had been built by William Toll many years before. He circled the village several times to alert the people to meet him at the airstrip across the Kamarang River from the village. He noted the beautiful country below—the village

Welcomed by smiling faces.

built on the peninsula, surrounded on three sides by the black but clean Kamarang, whose water was dark because of the trees and roots along its banks. Then he circled what had once been the campus of a school. He could see several small run-down buildings and a larger one that had been the missionaries' house. As a backdrop to the campus stood majestic Rain Mountain, and beyond, untouched rain forest.

As he landed he talked with God. "Give the people a vision. Now we see only desolation and ruins. No young people, just jungle. But You can change all that."

On the ground, David arranged a meeting with the town council of Paruima. Since they spoke a dialect he didn't know, he had brought along a friend, Albert Anthon, from Kaikan to interpret for him.

"Would you be willing to have a Bible training school here?" he asked the council.

"Yes, we would. But where will we find teachers?"

"The same place the money will come from. God will have to perform a miracle. But my question is, are you willing to do what it takes, to work hard?"

They thought a while. "We will charge for the trees we fell and the boards we cut," the spokesman said, and he named an amount.

"Hold it," David interrupted. "This is your project, not mine. I'm not coming in here with any money. If you want a school, you're going to build it! I will provide gasoline and chain saws, but you must build it. God will supply our needs."

"Well, we charge for our labor and . . ."

"No, no, no. We are not talking about charging for labor and making money. The question is, do you want this school, or do you not want it?"

The council members began talking among themselves. David's interpreter informed him of the trend in the conversation. They were discussing how each village had standard rates for services rendered, and how each must be paid. Again David interrupted.

"Look, folks, if we really want to build a school, this has to be a give-give and win-win relationship. You provide the labor and the boards. I'll provide the fuel and equipment. Frankly, I do not have the money now. I know God will supply all our needs. He always does. But if you will not provide the labor, I will go to another village."

The women, young people, and children standing around the town hall building had been listening intently. David began to hear those on the outside shouting through the open windows to the village council members. He asked Albert, "What are they saying?"

"The women keep saying to the men, 'Don't be stupid. We haven't had a school here for thirty years. If you don't do your part, we won't ever have a school here again.' "

With coaching from the people outside, it wasn't long until the men came to a decision. "We will give our labor. We will do our part."

"Great!" David exclaimed. "This will be a win-win solution as we work together with God." David shook hands with the council members as they smiled in agreement.

"Now let's plan together. First we need to repair the old, large house that was built in the 1950s. This will be adequate for the girls' dormitory and the women teachers. Then the smaller houses can become temporary dormitories for the boys, male teachers, and families. It looks as though the roofs leak and the floors might not be safe, but with your skills to repair them, they can be used for a while until we can build a larger building."

Prompted by David's vision and faith, they prayed that God would guide them to plan wisely. After a long discussion, David summarized the

First new building at Davis Indian Industrial College.

plans they had come up with.

"Our first building will have two stories. The upper floor will become the boys' dormitory at first, and the lower level will have three classrooms and two small teachers' offices. The second building will be a religion center, with classrooms for the Bible workers' training program and a chapel on the ground floor. The second floor will house the library and audiovisual center and another classroom."

One month before the ground breaking, the village workers cleared the construction site of brush and roped it off. On October 4, 1997, a large crowd filled the Seventh-day Adventist church on the hill above the river. At 3:00 P.M. some people walked the three-fourths of a mile along the trail from Paruima to the school, while others canoed upriver to the school construction site, all headed for the groundbreaking service.

David, the last speaker in the service, announced, "This school will focus on God's plan. All student labor and studies point to serving Christ through service for others. Remember, this is God's school. He is financing the entire project. Only as we go forward by faith will God make certain that the jar of oil does not run dry. Many youth from surrounding villages will have an opportunity to acquire academic and practical training in a Christ-centered environment. Please pray every day for this exciting project."

Construction began immediately. They cut down trees in the jungle and sawed them into rough lumber with the chain saws. Dragging the heavy, green boards for miles out of the jungle was backbreaking work, but the people of Paruima labored in love and faith that God would supply the means. All went well as funds continued to come in.

While work progressed on the school, David continued with his heavy flying schedule. The company back in Georgetown that supplied his aviation fuel allowed him to fill up as needed on condition that he pay his bill at the end of the month.

For several months sufficient funds came in to cover the fuel bill. Then came a month when, with a $1,000 fuel bill due in two days, David checked his bank balance and discovered only $200. He withdrew the funds and emailed his father to inquire if perhaps he had received some additional donations. The answer was negative, but it came with the encouraging news that they should make the matter a special subject of prayer that night. When David radioed back to Kaikan to ask for their prayers, his brother-in-law, Ted, chipped in with another

Paruima church

$100. Yet that was far from coming close to meeting the needed $1,000.

Puzzled, David prayed, "Lord, You have all resources. You could have supplied our needs before now. You know I don't have access to any funds except those You send me. If I don't get money to pay the bills, I'll be forced to ground the plane and halt the construction work in Paruima. Why would You bring us this far and then stop the work? Do You, who owns the cattle on a thousand hills, want word to spread to the villages that God was unable to provide the needed funds this month?"

Peace flooded David's mind as he remembered that "God has a thousand ways to provide for our needs, of which we know nothing." He slept well that night. Early in the morning he arose and began his worship. Again he prayed, "Lord, give me peace. You know I am very willing to stop the work if that is what You want me to do. However, I refuse to believe You have led us this far and then would allow the funds to stop."

He selected 1 Kings 17 for his study and read about Elijah and the widow and her renewed daily supply of oil. Suddenly a thought came to him. *Do like the widow, use what you have. But Lord,* he argued, *I don't need oil, I need cash.* He couldn't resist the overwhelming impression that he should at least count what he had. *It's no use,* he argued with himself.

I already know what I have. I just withdrew it from the bank. Because the conviction was so strong, he determined not to resist. He would simply count his money and prove the matter once and for all.

Becky and David walking to church with students

David opened his briefcase and took out the bank envelope. He was surprised to see many $20 bills and a couple of $100 bills he'd never seen before. He counted and recounted the money. He couldn't believe that the total was $1,050 in cash, more than enough to pay off the fuel bill.

David dropped on his knees, his heart overflowing with thanksgiving. "God, thank You for sending Your angels to put that money here. You have provided again." Opening his Bible, he read aloud, "Bless the Lord, O my soul, and forget not all his benefits: . . . Who satisfieth thy mouth with good things; so that thy youth is renewed like the eagle's" (Psalm 103:2, 5, KJV). "Praise the Lord for His goodness and wonderful mercies unto the children of men!" He radioed his family and emailed his father with news of the marvelous miracle. The young woman who received the funds to pay for the fuel commented, "Captain Gates, we love doing business with you because you always pay your bills." *God is honored when His children are able to pay their bills on time,* David thought to himself.

Six months later, David made an announcement to the surrounding community. "Prepare to start school. The temporary buildings have been repaired. Though the new building is not yet finished, God will provide the teachers soon."

"How can you start school with no teachers?" skeptical parents asked.

"I am learning a lesson from the Lord. It doesn't matter what you have or what you don't have. What matters is that you are doing what God wants you to do.

He is responsible for the consequences, not me and not you. Let's announce the opening day and see what God will do.

"Each morning the students and teachers will work on the farm, in the gardens, or cleaning on the campus, or in the kitchen. Parents will supply food till the gardens produce. They will attend classes in the afternoon to learn English, Spanish, religion, and music," David concluded.

Two weeks before school started, God impressed two young French couples the Gotins and the Mathieus, from Guadeloupe and Martinique to volunteer to teach under temporary conditions that first year. As the people saw how God had provided teachers, excitement ran high in Paruima.

Each villager dedicated one day a week to volunteer construction on the school. Seeing the end in sight, they set aside a full week in April to complete the final details of the two-story school building. Prospective students came four months early to plant the farm, clean the grounds, repair existing housing, and put up temporary thatch-roof buildings for cooking and storage. David flew in 200 pounds of rice, 100 pounds of split peas, and 100 pounds of flour, all donated, for the volunteers' noon meal. God must have smiled down on His happy children when they prepared for the dedication ceremonies for the first building.

A week later, Roland Thomson, the Caribbean Union treasurer, and other visitors from Andrews University flew to Paruima for the ground breaking of the religion center and library. Representing the Global Mission department of the Union, Thomson expressed his gratefulness for the work being done and presented a large financial gift from the Union to start the evangelistic work.

Round thatched Sabbath School rooms for the children.

After eighteen months of labor, the Davis Indian Industrial College at Paruima opened its doors officially in mid-October 1998 to thirty-one students, the only Adventist school in Guyana for thirty years. These dedicated pioneer students, carefully selected from many applicants, came from seven jungle villages. Four over-

seas faculty and three local staff members, all volunteers, dedicated themselves to giving these young missionaries-in-training a solid Christian education. Each student would work four hours in the morning and study for
four hours in the afternoon.

Because the school charged no tuition, a big question still loomed. "How
do we feed the students?" Most of the students were from jungle villages, and
the ones who came from Venezuela had walked a long distance across the
mountains, so they couldn't carry much food. Nor could their parents bring
food each week. Knowing God must have a plan, the missionaries prayed.

As David awoke the next morning, he remembered meeting a woman
called Norma Thomas, who as village captain for Kamarang, was also the
regional representative for SIMAP, a nongovernmental organization that provided food for labor to Amerindians who would improve their villages. David
went to visit her. When he shared the school's problem with her, she smiled.

"Captain Gates, last week we received over one hundred tons of food
from Norway, a wide variety of products. We are desperate to locate
projects where we can unload this large food deposit. I am sure our organization will approve this for the first year, before your farm begins to
produce. I will ask that we provide food for each student and also pay for
the charter flights necessary to fly it into Paruima."

Before the promised supplies began to arrive, food ran out at the
school. Students and staff prayed, asking God to supply their need. The
same day several canoes arrived carrying food sent by concerned parents.
Without dedicated parents, the students might have gone hungry. The
following week a plane arrived with seven hundred pounds of food. God
heard and answered the prayer.

During that first year David flew nearly a thousand hours. Bad weather
kept him grounded some days. He flew on Sabbath only in extreme medical emergencies or to meet a preaching appointment in a village. Thus, on
the days he flew, he spent from five to eight hours in the air, sometimes up
to seventeen flights in one day. At night he would fall asleep exhausted.

Who paid the fuel bills? God prompted many people to provide the
funds needed.

How did God use this small airplane to open doors for the gospel?
Many villages had hostile feelings against Seventh-day Adventists. In one
of the villages, the people would throw rocks at Adventist visitors until

they left the village. David sensed the same hostile attitude when he landed at that village to take a patient to the doctor. One day the pastor from the Wesleyan church in the village ventured near the airplane.

Before he took off, David called to him, "Pastor, would you be so kind to lead us in prayer before I take off?"

"Me?"

"Yes, you're a pastor, aren't you?"

"I am," he affirmed. "Shall we bow our heads in prayer as I ask God to bless Brother Gates, his airplane, and the patient."

After that the pastor came back regularly. David always asked him to pray.

Later the pastor of the Hallelujah church ventured to come close. David also asked him to pray. These continual contacts became more and more friendly. Finally, David asked if he could meet with the town council of this once hostile village.

"Would it be possible for me to bring to you a series of videos? We call them NET '95. Our Bible worker, also an Amerindian, will bring a video projector, a large screen, and a generator. The speaker, Mark Finley, presents Bible truths in a fascinating way. For five weeks we will show you a series of evangelistic sermons."

In the past the villagers might have thrown rocks at David, but now the town council voted "yes" unanimously. Afterwards, the Wesleyan pastor raised his hand. "I'll be willing to bring all the chairs from my church so they can have this meeting," he announced.

Each night the village people filled the town hall. At the conclusion of the video series, about a third of the people were baptized. Many of them came from the Wesleyan church, and the pastor seemed not to mind. He asked David,

"Do you think I could borrow your video projector someday?"

"Pastor, I'd be happy to loan it to you any time you need it." Thus God used respect, love, kindness, and the medical work of the airplane to open doors.

At home one evening at worship time, Becky said to David, "Already God has opened vast opportunities and challenges. We decided to test Him to see if He really keeps His promises. Truly, our family agrees with Paul in Romans 4:21, 'Being fully convinced that what He had promised He was also able to perform' " (NKJV).

CHAPTER 15

Trouble in the Dark

Several weeks later David and his oldest daughter, Katie, flew to Georgetown with a long list of "To Do" items. When the business was finished, they headed for the Guyana Conference administrative office for several hours of answering email correspondence. After dark they took a taxi to Davis Memorial Hospital, where they had accommodations for the night.

"Driver," David said, "please drop us off at the store a few blocks from the hospital. We need to buy something for supper."

With small bags of food in their arms and David holding on tightly to his briefcase, they hurried to cover the short distance to the hospital. David had walked that street many times, but now he felt extremely uncomfortable. Was his angel trying to tell him something? Ahead he saw three young men whom he'd seen before, the kind who often verbally harass those who pass by. Walking quickly, David looked back but saw no one following them.

As they rounded the corner and saw the light from the hospital, David relaxed and told Katie, "We're only about fifty feet from the hospital gate. I'm so thankful for our guardian angels that go with us through the darkness. I love the promise, 'The angel of the Lord encampeth around them that fear Him and delivereth them.' "

Seconds later, several blows from a club hit the back of David's head. He lost his balance and stumbled forward. Katie screamed as someone grabbed her from behind and hit her head. David tightened his grip on the briefcase as another man tried to jerk it from his hand. Food from the bags scattered around them. Glancing up, he saw the first man holding Katie with one hand and a wooden club in the other. Another blow slammed on the right side of his face. He recognized a man he'd seen as they walked. Katie screamed over and over. With his free hand, David grabbed her by the foot and held on. He felt that she must not be separated from him. He began to shout, "Help," hoping the security guards at the hospital would hear him.

Unable to snatch away David's briefcase, the second man began to search his pants pockets. Fortunately David had emptied them before walking down the dark street. Just then a car drove by, and the lights shone on them. Both men disappeared immediately. Two hospital security guards and some nurses heard the commotion and came running.

"Oh, it is you, Doctor Gates, and your daughter! We are so sorry." The "doctor" title came from David's years of teaching at Caribbean Union College in Trinidad.

They helped David and Katie inside, gave them first-aid treatment, and called the police. By the time three officers arrived, the pain in David's head had begun to lessen. Dr. Lara filled out medical forms.

"Are you able to go with us in the pickup truck to identify where you purchased the food and the path you walked?" a police officer asked.

"Yes, I think so."

As the police truck reached the entrance to the road a block away, David saw the same three young men standing around as if nothing had happened.

Pointing to them, David whispered, "Those are the guys who assaulted us."

Quickly stopping the truck, the police ordered them into the back and headed for the police station. Under better light, David identified two of them as his assailants. Though they denied involvement, David gave a full statement of all that had happened. The third suspect was released, and the other two taken into custody.

"I'm very tired and don't feel good. It's 1:00 A.M. Please take me to the hospital so I can sleep."

"We'll be glad to do so if you will return tomorrow with your daughter for further investigation."

The next morning after breakfast the security guard who had seen the men illuminated by the car lights, along with Katie and David, took a taxi to the police station. The police took each of them separately into a room where the assailants sat. Guyana law requires that the accuser must identify the accused by stepping forward and touching the person. This procedure terrified Katie, who broke down under the stress. She started to cry and couldn't answer the many questions. David prayed, "Give her courage, Lord."

The police officer allowed David to come into the room to help her. After a few minutes she regained her composure, finished her statement, and signed it.

After the ordeal they went to a juice shop, collapsed into chairs, and regained their energy drinking pineapple and cherry juice.

"Daddy, why didn't our angels intervene last night?" Katie asked.

"Muffin, sometimes God allows pain and loss. I cannot answer your question why. But someday we will understand, like Job did, that God's sustaining power never fails when we simply trust Him. He didn't leave us nor forsake us even though we both felt the blows on our heads and we've got bruises. Let's pray like Jeremiah did: 'Heal me, O Lord, and I shall be healed; save me, and I shall be saved: for thou art my praise' " (Jeremiah 17:14, KJV).

CHAPTER 16

Life in a Jungle Village

David and Becky faced the constant danger of the worst parasitic disease in the tropics—malaria. This terrible disease had become almost an epidemic in Kaikan. To complicate matters they had to determine which of the two main types of malaria the patient was suffering from in order to give the correct treatment. *Plasmodium vivax* responded to chloroquine and primaquine, but *Plasmodium falciparum,* a much more serious and often fatal type, needed quinine and other drugs.

One night about midnight they awoke to someone pounding on the door. A worried voice called out, "Ingrid is vomiting again."

"I'll come right away," Becky's mother answered.

"I'll go with you, Mom." The two of them put on pants and shoes for protection against snakes.

A new villager, Errol, and his common-law wife, Ingrid, the parents of one-year-old Tyza and two-month-old baby Nicoleta, had come to Kaikan village a few months before to stay with Errol's sister, Lucita, and her husband, Freeman, who had three children. They all lived in a small house about 9 feet wide by 12 feet long.

Ingrid was suffering from a serious case of malaria. She was so ill that she couldn't nurse her baby. Soon little Tyza was bitten and infected, and then Freeman, Lucita's husband. Previously Freeman had been sick for

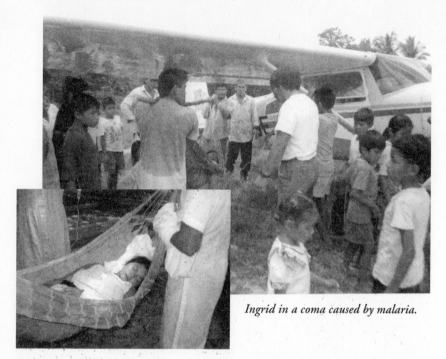

Ingrid in a coma caused by malaria.

months. He had become so weak and jaundiced that David had flown him to the Georgetown government hospital. Now Freeman was suffering a relapse and was shaking like a leaf from the chills.

With so many sick, Lucita's small house seemed like a hospital. Ingrid vomited repeatedly. Little Tyza was burning up with fever. Since Ingrid couldn't keep the medication down, Becky and her mother, Patti, started intravenous fluids.

The next morning Ingrid seemed better, but Freeman's weakness made him unable to walk to the runway. Because no one knew what time David would return from the flight he was making, two men strung up a hammock on a long pole and carried Freeman to the medical building near the runway. David returned too late to fly him to Georgetown that night. Florencia Peters, the local community health worker, fixed a place for him to rest, and Lucita spent the night with him. Errol stayed with Ingrid and the children at the house.

When Ingrid began vomiting again, Errol left them and in desperation ran to the Gateses' house not far away. Without even a flashlight on a very dark night, he managed to follow the path and didn't step on any snakes.

Becky's mother ran with Errol back to the house. As Ingrid rolled over for the injection, she gasped, "I feel so sick. I just don't think I can make it."

Early the next morning David left for Georgetown with Freeman. About an hour later Becky checked on Ingrid. Since she had not vomited, Becky gave her pills, wondering why she seemed unusually drowsy.

Because of all the malaria cases in Kaikan, David had flown in a health worker to do blood smears on everyone. The health worker stood talking to Becky and her mother under the mango tree by their house when Lucita's little boy came running. A few moments later they heard wailing sounds. A stab of fear pierced Becky's heart. Not taking time to find her sandals, she ran barefoot, praying as she went. Her mother followed close behind. The people crowding the doorway let Becky in. Errol screamed hysterically, "She's dying! She's dying! Oh Ingrid, please don't die! I'll marry you, Ingrid, if only you will get better."

"Her vital signs and color are good," Becky's mother whispered. A quick glance told them Ingrid was unconscious in her hammock. Putting her arms around Errol's shoulders, Becky asked, "I don't know if you are a Christian, but may I pray to God for Ingrid?"

"Oh, yes," he quickly agreed. During the prayer he settled down.

Becky ran back home and placed an urgent call on the radio. "David, come back as soon as you drop off Freeman. We have another critically ill patient." Two and a half hours later, she heard him taxi up the runway.

Errol and another man again strung up the hammock on a pole. Holding the IV bag as they walked to the plane, Becky shaded Ingrid's pale face with an umbrella. David pushed the passenger seat all the way back, strapped Errol in with the jump-seat seat belt, and padded the floor with a sleeping bag. They laid Ingrid with her head on Errol's lap and strapped her in with the passenger seat belt. David tied the IV bag to a hook on the ceiling.

The little group gathered around the plane, asking God for guidance and healing power. After David took off, Becky radioed a friend to meet the plane and take the unconscious passenger to the hospital. Then she and her girls took Ingrid's two babies home until Lucita, who taught school each morning, could come home and care for them.

The family rejoiced as they heard the plane return just before sunset on that Friday evening. As they gathered for Sabbath worship, Becky prayed, "How can we thank You, God, for that little airplane that provides life and help for these dear people. We have great joy, as Jesus did, helping with their physical problems. Now, God, may they learn of Your great love for them."

Ted Burgdorff treats Leif Aaen, one of our student missionaries, after he was bitten by a poisonous snake.

Two days later a radio report came that Ingrid was somewhat better, but Errol now had a high fever from malaria.

During the next few weeks the evil angels seemed to delight in planning a series of problems for the missionaries. David and Becky offered to help some villagers harvest their crops. As David and Becky followed the villagers through the jungle, David swung his sharp machete. Suddenly he hit his knee, cutting clear through his jeans. Five stitches closed the wound.

The same day, Leif, the student missionary from Andrews University who had copiloted the plane to Guyana with David, was playing with the kids in the river. He dived in and hit his head on a sharp object that cut a large gash in his forehead.

A short time later, Ted, using a chisel on some woodwork, hit a knot. The chisel slipped and sliced across two fingers on his left hand. One of those fingers already had a bite of unknown origin that had begun to swell and looked infected. The finger, swollen to twice its normal size, didn't respond to antibiotic ointment or hydrotherapy. By the third day there were red streaks running up his arm. His lymph nodes felt hard. Deeply concerned, his wife, Betsy, prayed as she applied continuous charcoal poultices. Still the finger got worse. On the fourth day the finger began to drain and the red streaks receded. Three weeks later the swelling had gone down, but the skin still looked purple. Another several weeks went by before the finger looked normal. The native people thought a scorpion, a centipede, or a spider had caused the trouble.

The crowning act in this series of accidents came as a group left home for Friday evening vespers at the church. Leif, walking some distance behind the main group, noticed a piece of gray cloth as he climbed the hill. *I'm going to get rid of that,* he thought. *It looks like a snake and might frighten someone.* He picked up the cloth, took a few steps off the trail, and tossed it away. Wearing only sandals, he stepped on a poisonous snake, a pit viper, hidden in the grass, and felt a bite on his toe.

Hearing Leif's shout, Ted ran back and immediately began to suck the wound. One of the children ran to the house for charcoal and an ace bandage to use as a tourniquet. The adults in the group picked up Leif and carried him back to the house.

God must have arranged, a few days before, for Ted to read an Internet news bulletin sent by a friend about the use of shock treatment for snakebite. He had shared it with the family, and they discussed it at length. Thinking about what he had read so recently, Ted connected a wire to the ignition of the gas-powered weed trimmer and began to give Leif small amounts of electric shock at fifteen-minute intervals, beginning at the site of the bite and widening the area as time went on.

Since there is no antivenin for snakebite anywhere in Guyana, charcoal treatment was all they could do. Leif was suffering severe pain, but each time they applied the charcoal paste he felt relief. When the pain returned, they applied fresh charcoal, and the pain subsided. Over and over that night they repeated the charcoal poultices.

Word quickly spread by the jungle grapevine. Soon half of the church had gathered and surrounded Leif, seeing firsthand how to treat snakebite. The people prayed that God would spare Leif's life. During that evening as they treated the young man, four snakes were killed and brought to the house within two hours. The devil, like the Israelites in the wilderness, seemed out to get God's people. But God is greater than the enemy in this world.

Sabbath morning Leif walked on the bitten foot with just a little pain, an unheard-of thing. If victims of pit viper bites stay alive, they usually have pain and swelling for several months afterwards. Leif didn't even have any swelling. God sent His energy, His power, and His wisdom to those who provided quick treatment. Natural remedies had produced the most remarkable recovery from a poisonous-snake bite that they had ever witnessed.

However, Satan wasn't finished with the harassment. A cunning and experienced hunter began sneaking up on the dogs in Kaikan. In a short time, the killer, a jaguar, had killed nineteen of them. No one felt safe, especially not the children. Extremely bold, the jaguar had entered the kitchen of a village house and dragged out the household dog after paralyzing it with a paw swipe. School children arriving early at school noticed the jaguar run out of the school building, where it had been sleeping. Obviously the cat had lost its fear of human beings. Children were at risk.

The village people found a dog half eaten by the jaguar. They urged the village policeman to help them, since he had a gun.

"I'm going to get that jaguar," he promised. "I'll take the half-eaten dog and set up a blind in a tree close by. I need one of the village men with me."

The two men stayed in the blind all day. Around six in the evening, the villagers heard a gunshot, then a few seconds later another shot. Someone came running.

"She's dead. Come and see her. She's a big one," the messenger announced.

The kids donned boots and long pants to protect themselves from snakes, grabbed their flashlights and their moms and dads, and rushed to see the creature. Old but still beautiful, her teeth were worn down, which made it impossible for her to bring down bigger animals. After the villagers had skinned her, they gave her meat to the few remaining dogs that had survived her hunting. Several nights later they heard another jaguar call, presumably her mate or her cub. After that night no one heard or saw another jaguar.

A few days later a couple of boys brought in a ten-foot-long boa constrictor, as big around as a man's thigh. It puffed itself up and let out ominous hissing sounds when anyone came close. They tied "Mr. Hiss" to Becky's wash table. She refused to wash any more clothes until they moved the huge creature. David put the snake in a bag in the luggage compartment of the plane to take to the zoo in Georgetown.

Becky looked worried. "David, aren't you afraid that thing will get out of the bag, grab you, and strangle you in mid-air?"

David came close and gave her a big hug. "I'm so glad, Sweetie-pie, that you care about this pilot. I put it in a double bag and tied an extra rope around the top of the bag. I didn't want to give my angel any extra challenges."

In Georgetown, David usually stayed at the home of the hospital medical director and her husband—Dr. Faye Whiting-Jensen and her husband Steve. When David arrived at the apartment, no one was home, so he left the double-bagged snake on the porch and left for about an hour. When he came back, David heard shouting and a great commotion on the porch. Steve and the hospital's general surgeon, Dr. Arsenio Gonzales, were standing on the sofa with sticks, trying to hold down the big snake.

"Oh, there's Mr. Hiss, my snake that I'm taking to the zoo," David exclaimed. He reached down, grabbed it by the back of the head, and deposited it securely in the bag. So that's how that snake got up here," exclaimed Steve. "We couldn't figure out how such a large snake could find its way up the stairs and onto the porch."

A few days later a man knocked on the door of the Gateses' house back in Kaikan. He had hiked seven hours at night through the jungle from the village of Arau.

"Please help. Eight-year-old Daniel is very sick because a snake bit him."

"I'm so glad they've completed the airstrip there," David called as he ran to the plane. What took seven hours by jungle trail would take only seven minutes in the plane. Rushing into the home where the boy lay, David's heart sank as he saw how grossly swollen little Daniel's leg looked. He also noticed that his gums had already started to bleed. He doubted that little Daniel would survive.

David gathered the village folk together for prayer. He dedicated the little boy to God should his life be spared. He continued to pray as he flew him to the government-run clinic at Kamarang. They had no medicines but immediately got a plane to fly Daniel to Georgetown.

God answered those prayers. Daniel survived and returned home to Arau. But he continued to have swelling and an ugly wound, so again David flew him out of Arau, this time to Kaikan and Becky's good nursing care. She repeatedly soaked his foot, plastered it with antibacterial cream, and bandaged it. Finally his foot returned to normal.

Often Becky praised her Divine Helper. "Thank You, Jesus. Your healing power is evident here in these jungle villages. Over and over we experience your promise, 'Who forgiveth all thine iniquities; who healeth all thy diseases' " (Psalm 103:3, KJV).

CHAPTER 17

The Jordan River Parts

For two weeks David had kept in close touch with the Ministry of Health in Guyana. The temporary permission to operate his aircraft in the interior would expire on October 31, 1997. He visited the director of regional services and spoke to the physician in charge of all medical care in Guyana's interior.

The physician told him, "I have heard much of the work you are doing for the people in the villages. I promise to get the needed letter of recommendation to the Ministry of Health within three days."

Daily telephone calls to his secretary and visits to the Ministry of Health revealed he had not come through with his promise. In fact, he seemed to be avoiding both David and David's friend, Winston James, who was director of education for the Guyana Conference of Seventh-day Adventists and David's assistant in the aviation program in Georgetown.

"I fear the plane will be grounded until that letter is acquired," Winston said, looking discouraged.

"Winston, please call the DCA (director of civil aviation) and tell him all that we've done to comply with his request. Maybe he'll understand and allow the plane to fly," David said. "I know God has acted as our prayers ascended these two weeks. I'm sure He has commissioned a mighty army of angels to do His work. He promised to send 'His angels, who excel in strength, who do His word, heeding the voice of His word … [and] do His pleasure' (Psalm 103:20, 21, NKJV). This aviation program is His. I choose to trust Him for His solution."

The next day, October 31, David called Winston to find out the result. His voice sounded ecstatic. "The DCA couldn't believe that all our efforts had produced nothing. He encouraged us to keep flying and not to let this bother us. He even added, 'If the Ministry of Health doesn't want to help you, I happen to know someone much higher who will certainly give you support. You need to arrange an appointment with the Prime Minister, Janet Jagan, herself. I know she'll support your work.' "

"Did you tell the DCA that seven visitors from the United States will arrive next week? Does he know their plan to develop health and education projects in the interior through ADRA? Did you mention that the Michigan physician who's been covering for Davis Memorial Hospital has accepted our invitation to do medical work in the villages for four days before he returns to the U.S.?"

"Yes, I told him all that. He suggested that even though the permit technically expires today, to keep flying. He wants you to take these visitors to the villages. But he emphasized the need to get the appointment with the Prime Minister soon, so she can continue to give support in the future."

"Winston, this is exciting," David said. "God's plans far exceed ours. The Prime Minister is running for president next year. Imagine Guyana's soon-to-be CEO supporting our program. It's surely great to be in partnership with God."

By 3:00 A.M. on November 4, all seven visitors had arrived safely and were in bed by 4:30. Several hours later, after breakfast, David rushed to the bank to cash a check to pay for the chartered plane that would take five of the visitors to the school in Paruima. From there he took a taxi to the conference office to meet Winston James. Together they would go to the Minister of Amerindian Affairs to get permission for the visitors to travel into the interior.

Stepping into the office, he overheard Winston talking to the director of civil aviation on the phone. Phrases like "the plane is grounded" hit David hard. The promised letter from the Ministry of Health was almost blank. Without the ministry's recommendation, the DCA could not renew the permit. The mission plane was grounded.

"May I speak to him?" David asked. Winston handed him the phone.

"I can understand the difficult position you are in. However, may I explain to you that our purpose this past year has been building up to this climax? These visitors have been invited to survey the work that has been done, and to offer tangible help in health, education, improved lifestyle and benefits to the people living in the interior. They represent a worldwide organization called ADRA, or Adventist Development and Relief Agency. They provide help from drilling fresh-water wells to teaching the people industrial skills. Whatever projects they propose will be forwarded to ADRA International headquarters for funding. Could it be that the problem that has grounded our plane, the only way into remote communities, has been caused by the enemy who hates doing good for needy people?"

The DCA agreed. Praying in his heart, David continued.

"Would you be willing to extend our permit for seven days, long enough to transport these visitors?"

"No, I cannot." David's silent prayers continued.

"Would you be willing to present our request to the Transportation Board?"

"Strange you should mention this, because they meet only once a month. It just so happens that the meeting convenes this afternoon."

David's heart began to pound with hope. "Sir, I am convinced this is no coincidence. Obviously God is taking control. We will be praying that when you present the great need for the use of this plane, they will give their approval."

The DCA answered, "Keep up your prayers. It will take all the power of God to convince those men to make an exception."

After hanging up, David and Winston asked the ADRA visitors to join them in the conference president's office. "I have bad news," David said. "The plane is grounded. But the good news is that our God, who has clearly led in the past, is able to do so now. Let us kneel in a prayer circle and ask that they will grant even more than the seven-day extension we asked for."

Earnest prayers went up to God asking that He use His strong arm of deliverance. Peace filled every heart.

"Let's proceed with our previous plans," David said when they were finished. "The chartered plane is waiting to take you to the interior now. I know God has already answered our prayers. By His grace, we will join you tomorrow."

After they left, David and Winston went to the Prime Minister's office and began making arrangements for an appointment as soon as possible. Next they visited with the Minister of Amerindian Affairs.

"Our village captains from the interior have given us favorable reports of your work. I plan to write letters to both the Minister of Health and the DCA giving our approval of your health and education projects. I am glad to give travel approval to your visitors from the United States."

Winston and David thanked the minister and left. At 3:45 P.M. they called the DCA just as he was returning to his office from the board meeting. "The current of favor has swung your way again," he said. "After much discussion, we agreed to extend the time of your permit for ten days."

David's voice sounded jubilant. "Thank you so much. Clearly God is in control. He used you to answer our prayers."

As they lifted off the next morning David and Winston sang together, "Praise God from whom all blessings flow."

"Because of His abundant grace we have all been blessed time and time again," Winston exclaimed.

God used the little plane to give the visitors an understanding of the Amerindians' needs. Several isolated communities benefited. Arau needed a primary school. ADRA assisted and helped to complete the school. ADRA also provided some materials for the Davis Indian Industrial College in Paruima, and arranged to supply food for the villagers donating voluntary labor for the school. Over the years, Christian kindness, combined with health care and education, have developed close friendships in villages previously unfriendly to Adventists.

Near the end of the ten days of flying permission, David received a number of radio calls from the Guyana Defense Force military base twenty-five miles north of Kaikan. Nineteen soldiers were suffering from malaria. David took blood samples to Kamarang for microscope analysis to determine the appropriate medication needed for each soldier. Four additional mercy flights saved the lives of seriously ill patients in other villages. Tired but blessed, David flew nearly 100 hours that month.

During the dry season it had always been hard to find potable water. One patient David had transported was stricken with typhoid fever from a polluted source of water. David thanked God for the ADRA projects that could provide clean, pure drinking water from wells in the future.

He thought of another blessing that would come through their program—disease prevention. To make this challenging task happen, they would use modern technology to lure the villagers—a video projector, a VCR, a small generator, and a large screen. Videos on health education, in English but accompanied by Amerindians translating in the Akawayo or Arecuna dialects, would attract the entire village.

After David had flown the ADRA visitors back to Georgetown, he and Becky reflected on God's ability to deal with the unknown. One year before they had stepped out in faith into an uncertain future with no funds of their own. What had happened when they depended entirely on God? Housing, a balanced diet for their family, a small bush plane, operating permits and funds, new runways in isolated villages, miraculous multiplication of funds to pay bills, and a boarding industrial school, had all been provided. To top it off, they had just learned that their daughters had received full scholarships in an excellent boarding academy in the United States.

Can God be trusted to provide for His children? Absolutely!

Too soon the ten days of flying permission expired.

"Becky, let's sit down and talk." Putting his arm around her, David announced, "I must leave, Sweetie-pie. The grounded plane has to be parked at the Georgetown airport. I'll schedule the plane for maintenance during this down time. I've been asked as the volunteer director of ADRA Guyana to participate in a one-week seminar on disaster preparedness."

"Where and for whom?" she asked.

"On the island of Antigua. They've invited ADRA leaders from the

Caribbean, West Indies, and French-Antilles Unions. I hate to leave you alone so long with Carlos and Kris, but I'll try to keep in touch by radio."

During that time he used a solar-powered battery charger and a portable battery to make two daily radio contacts with Becky. Far away in the jungles of Guyana, she had to deal with several very ill village children suffering from advanced malaria. She noted that malaria medications were running low.

The next time David contacted her, she said, "I need you, David. With half our family away, the boys and I feel so lonely here. Many of the patients need a doctor, not just a nurse. I'm thankful we have Jesus here with us."

As soon as he returned to Guyana, David contacted the director of civil aviation. "Sorry, but the communication from the minister is that the plane may not leave the ground until further notice and that could be a long time."

Desperate to join Becky, David and Winston kept up their prayer vigil. "We've got a mighty promise here. Listen, Winston. 'We have no might against this great company that cometh against us; neither know we what to do: but *our eyes are upon thee....* Thus saith the Lord unto you, Be not afraid nor dismayed by reason of this great multitude; for the battle is not yours, but God's' " (2 Chronicles 20:12, 15, KJV; italics supplied).

Still, David's daily visits to civil aviation always resulted in a disinterested response: "No word yet."

Radio contact with Becky added to his concern. She told him, "Yesterday afternoon the captain from the village of Arau hiked seven hours to Kaikan looking for malaria medications for some of the villagers, including our own native missionaries there. All I could do was pray and shed tears of frustration at being unable to provide medications to adequately treat these people we love. If only you could fly them in."

David claimed the wonderful promise, "Our heavenly Father has a thousand ways to provide for us, of which we know nothing. Those who accept the one principle of making the service and honor of God supreme will find perplexities vanish, and a plain path before their feet" (*The Desire of Ages*, p. 330).

The next day as David and Winston drove to the airport to do some work on the plane, they prayed for guidance. "Lord, please show us what You want us to do."

Suddenly God's answer began to develop clearly in David's mind.

"Prepare for expansion! Winston, I'm impressed that this delay must be God's call to move forward more aggressively. He's telling us to expand to new regions where requests for Bible workers and medical care have been coming in for years."

"But, David, that means a larger aircraft and unrestricted access to Guyana's interior. I'm sure you understand that with the increased flexibility and freedom we'll need, our operating costs will skyrocket. And who will fly a second plane?"

"I know the problems. That's the beauty of this whole plan. Funding for the program has always rested completely on God. Moving forward at God's bidding would automatically result in an increase of available resources. Isn't it thrilling! Every advance by faith turns out to be a Jordan River experience, which builds our confidence that indeed the battle is the Lord's, not ours."

Overwhelmed with the Spirit of the Lord, David stopped the car. The two men bowed their heads. With tears of joy flowing down their cheeks, they prayed, "God, we commit our plans into Your hands. Please give us success with the people involved. Increase our funding as a sign that we are moving in the right direction."

Winston added, "Precious Father, we feel as if we are standing on Jordan's riverbank with our feet about to touch the water."

Early the next morning, David called the air taxi company and explained his plan. "Impossible! The insurance company would never allow it."

"Please let me speak with the general manager," David asked.

"No, not now, but I'll pass on the message."

That afternoon someone from the air taxi company called. "Please give us a letter explaining your proposal in detail. Also include your pilot's resume." David acted promptly. At the airport he met the air taxi's chief pilot. "I like your idea," he said, nodding his head.

The following day David received a message. "Come right away to speak with the managing director and the general manager."

The men greeted David with interest as he stepped into the office.

"We know about your medical program, but we have a few questions about your past flight experience in the Caribbean and abroad. Your request is to be included on our insurance as a company pilot and to use one of our Cessna 206s. This is of interest to us. We find the proposal attractive."

David's heart beat faster as he listened. "We're especially interested in the fact that you have a Piper Seneca type rating on your Guyana commercial pilot license. As you know, we have a Seneca that we frequently can't fly because we only have a few qualified pilots with Seneca type ratings. We'll help you out with the Cessna 206 if you'll help us by flying the Seneca on occasional international flights. We request that you cover the cost of the check flight to Kaikan in the 206 with our chief pilot. Later, we will check you out on the Seneca."

David could hardly repress his elation as he summarized the proposal. "Am I clear that I'll have a couple of local aircraft to add to the flexibility of our medical mission program without any restrictions? Will I be performing as temporary company pilot of the air taxi agency?"

"Yes, you will be allowed to fly anywhere in the country, but first you must coordinate your plans with the chief pilot for approval."

"Thank you so much. This will certainly make it easier and cheaper to handle larger groups of visitors as I take them into the interior."

David felt as if he were walking on air as he left the office. "God, the Jordan River has begun to part!"

Then the reality of his situation hit home. His funds from the U.S. for January had already come through, and he had committed them for school construction in Paruima. He didn't have enough money left to pay the rent for the 206 checkout. *What do I do now, God?* he thought. The promise in Psalm 46:10 flashed into his mind: "Be still, and know that I am God" (KJV).

I'll obey, God. I'll say nothing about my lack of money. But I'm a bit scared to commit funds that would put me beyond the limit of meeting current needs. Nevertheless, Your biddings are enablings, so I'll go ahead and schedule the flight for Sunday.

He thought that he could also take advantage of the trip to fly the four members of the mission team into the interior—Katie, his oldest daughter; Julie, a student missionary; and a French couple who were coming to teach in Paruima. He would need new funds that week to break even, since he was not expecting any deposits for another three weeks.

Thank You for letting me talk over my problems with You, the great God of the universe. Now I leave everything in Your hands.

On his way, David stopped to check his email. He read the one from his father first.

Dear Son,

Last night, Helen Fisher, our church treasurer at Marion, Illinois told me that since she was leaving on vacation, she had made arrangements to send in the available funds a bit early to our Guyana account. They have been deposited for your use.

In reverence David dropped to his knees. "What a wonderful God You are! You arranged that nearly a whole month's worth of funding became available within an hour after I scheduled the plane checkout. *The Jordan River has completely parted once again!* 'Make a joyful noise unto God, all ye lands: Sing forth the honour of his name: make his praise glorious'" (Psalm 66:1, 2, KJV).

David paused.

"But, God, I know I cannot weary You. Our small medical plane still sits on the ground. You are aware that our planned evangelistic work will be almost impossible without our small plane on those jungle runways. Many sick people with life-threatening health problems need transportation. I can't stay in the interior without that plane. Our eyes are upon You. You will do it, I know."

CHAPTER 18

Surprises and Sickness

A new minister of health had been appointed. Would he give his approval when the previous minister had refused? As they went to see him, David and Winston asked that God would give them favor in his eyes.

First they stopped to meet the minister of regional development. Winston recognized him immediately. They had been kids growing up together. His friendliness gave them courage.

"I have a vital interest in seeing development in the interior. You can be assured of my complete support with your projects."

A rumor was circulating that the new minister of health had been raised as a Seventh-day Adventist but had turned against religion many years before. With another word of prayer, they entered his office.

He sat with arms crossed. His unfriendly tone showed annoyance. "I agreed to support your program in the cabinet meeting yesterday, but I have no idea what it is all about."

David smiled and said, "I'll be glad to inform you. We're working in the interior to develop a partnership with your ministry. We want to be called on when opportunities develop for vaccinations and other emergencies. Our goal is that you will consider us a valuable asset, a means of helping to improve the health of Guyana's residents in the interior."

The minister smiled and seemed to relax. "Do you use our radio frequency?" he asked.

"No, we have not received proper authorization." David watched him scribble something on a notepad.

"I'll send a letter of authorization that will allow your base and plane to communicate directly with the regional hospital and the ministry. I've already given my support to the minister overseeing the Department of Civil Aviation. Should you need further help, just let me know."

Thrilled at the marked change of attitude, David asked, "May we have a word of prayer with you, asking God's blessing on your leadership?" The minister consented.

A few hours later a representative in the Department of Civil Aviation called. "Your permit has been renewed. Come and pick up the written authorization as soon as possible. Since your plane has a foreign registration, you will have to operate on three-month permits up to a maximum of a year."

With joy David flew into his home airstrip at Kaikan for Sabbath. After he shared the blessings of God's leadership with his family, he added, "Now we must pray, trust, and wait for God to provide a permanent four-seat aircraft that can be locally registered."

"I think He has already given us the answer," Becky said as she opened her Bible. " 'Now unto him that is able to do exceeding abundantly above all that we ask or think, according to the power that worketh in us, unto him be glory in the church by Christ Jesus through all ages, world without end' " (Ephesians 3:20, 21, KJV).

Word spread among the villages that the plane was operating again. The number of calls for mercy flights from isolated villages grew quickly. The village of Phillippi, near the Brazilian border, had had an Adventist church in the past. It had fallen into disrepair, and many of the villagers belonged to two denominations with hostile feelings. Because of drought and a lack of river transportation, bringing in a sick person for help took more than four days. When David flew three seriously ill villagers to the hospital, he received a heart-warming response from formerly hostile people and their village captain.

"If I brought the video equipment, would you show videos on health and the life of Christ?" he asked them.

"Yes, please do." A dozen voices behind him shouted, "Yes, yes."

A district pastor visited the people when David showed the videos. Walls of separation began to crumble. They agreed to show the five-week evangelistic campaign called NET '95. In response, the people of Phillippi have rebuilt the church, bigger than before.

Two more villages, Paruima and Waramadong, which already had some Adventist members, asked for the NET '95 series. A total of sixty-five people chose to accept Jesus and asked to be baptized in Paruima, and another group followed suit in Waramadong. Phillippi and Chinowieng had very few Adventist members. As David flew around the region performing medical care, he brought fuel for the generators and food for the support team doing evangelistic work in those villages.

Arau had become a village only five years before. The members there begged for a primary school. Classes began with three volunteers—Beverly Godette, a Guyanese teacher, Katie, David's daughter, and her good friend Julie Christman, the student missionary. But the older village folk begged, "Please, let us go to school. All our life we've wanted to read. May we come too?"

"I'm so sorry," David said, "but there just isn't room, nor are there teachers available for so many."

Disturbed at refusing them, David and Becky prayed for an idea. Christians could attend day classes and become Bible workers, but what to do with those who were not Christians? They needed help too.

"Maybe we could put up a small community TV station run by solar charges. A hundred watts of power would reach about fifteen miles, which could include three or four of the eight villages in the Upper Mazaruni River district. The whole village could pool their resources and buy one solar panel, a battery, and one television. Then everyone could come and watch."

"Sounds great. With no other channels to watch but our Christian station, we could beat the devil at his own game," Becky said with a laugh. "The village people would enjoy programs both in dialect and English using nature, health, and religious videos. But where can you get permission to operate this?"

"From the government, from the new Prime Minister, Samuel Hinds himself. I must stop at his office and get details from his secretary."

The secretary informed David, "You must collect signatures from all the village leaders and people. Unless they want what you have to offer, your request will not be considered."

A month later David had arranged a meeting for all of the religious leaders and all the captains or chiefs of the eight villages in the area around Kaikan. He explained what he planned to do with the TV station. They listened carefully. "If you want this, you must sign these papers."

The first person that stood up, an Anglican priest, took his pen and said, "I want to be the first to sign that we want Adventist television here."

He started the trend. The other ministers followed. Soon the teachers and the village captains joined. Everyone present eagerly signed the petition.

David took the pages of signatures to the office of the Prime Minister. He never expected such unanimous approval, but David knew the influence of the medical and educational work had brought trust and a change in attitude. The signers added one stipulation: "We will only allow this TV station if David Gates is in charge of the operations, or someone he approves."

Amidst all these blessings at the spread of the gospel, Satan showed his hate by aiming a deadly weapon at the people—mosquitoes. Another epidemic of malaria struck, not only in Kaikan, but many surrounding villages. Three times in three weeks David's family was confined to bed with fever, chills, headache, and nausea. David recovered from *P. Falciparum,* but then Becky got it from a single mosquito that somehow got into the mosquito net. He promptly got *P. Vivax.* After taking medication he began to recover, and then Becky became ill again. All the families of the village suffered this way. As soon as one felt better, another family member got sick. Something would have to be done!

Two malaria officers spent three weeks in Kaikan treating more than one hundred patients. However, family members kept re-infecting each other. David contacted ADRA for emergency funds. Because it was difficult to get patients to take multiple treatments of medication, they opted for an expensive but effective one-time treatment called Mefloquin, a single dose of which wipes out multiple types of malaria. ADRA Canada and ADRA Holland approved the funding so that everyone in the village could take this medication at the same time. As an added precaution, two shipments of treated mosquito nets made especially for hammocks arrived from the Ministry of Health. Local people were trained and materials provided so that hammock-style mosquito nets could be made.

The Ministry of Amerindian Affairs loaned David a fogger machine to spray the houses with insecticide and vegetable oil, the latter to assure the walls would hold the insecticide. Cockroaches, bugs, and mosquitoes dropped dead after the spray. Each day the people found dead insects on the floor and table. Filled with hope, the villagers prayed that this triple approach would eradicate the serious malaria threat.

David flew to the village of Arau and discovered that almost all the residents had come down with malaria. Would the epidemic ever end? Dr. Faye Whiting-Jensen, medical director for Davis Memorial hospital, flew in to Arau with David and personally supervised the mass treatment of all residents. The results were a resounding success. Arau became the only village with no reported cases of malaria during the rest of the epidemic.

The loving attention poured out on so many sick persons also resulted in spiritual growth for many. David smiled. "We surely keep God busy working on the miracle of human hearts. Soon the three-month operating permit for our little plane will expire. More volunteers will arrive for work in the interior at that time." David paused and looked heavenward. "God, we wait upon You! I'm sure You'll come through just in time."

As usual, the dependable God who delights in bringing joy to His children did come through. On June 11 David received a phone call from the Civil Aviation office. "Your flight permit on the Cessna has been renewed for another three months."

David shared his joy with Becky, and then he mentioned a need that was on his mind. "I do hope that when God impresses the right people to volunteer as an aviation mechanic and also a professional pilot that they'll come to assist me with the workload."

"God will provide in His own time," Becky assured him. She always spoke with faith. "Could it be that God keeps us in heaven's waiting room to perfect our faith? But for now I rejoice that the Davis Indian Industrial College is debt free. And next week we'll break ground for the religion center and library. Our cup is running over."

"Indeed it is," David said. "Each day we face further challenges as God opens a new vista in His plans for Guyana. I wonder what's next on His agenda."

CHAPTER 19

God Pushes Forward

Returning from Georgetown, David hurried from the runway to his house. Rushing down the sloping path, he called from the door, "Becky, where are you? God is doing exciting things again!"

Coming down the stairs, she met him with a hug and a kiss. "Please sit down before you fall down," she said. "I'm listening."

"Remember I told you about the large beacon tower next to the runway in Kamarang owned by Civil Aviation? Well, they're willing to allow us to lease a space on the tower where we can place a TV broadcast antenna. God impressed me to send in an application form and ask for an appointment with the Prime Minister to discuss getting a TV station broadcast license for Kamarang."

"So what happened?"

"The Prime Minister arrived forty-five minutes late. The security scanned us with their metal scanner and checked us for weapons. Finally they escorted Winston and me into the Prime Minister's office. Standing by his desk, he looked angry as he shuffled some papers. Without looking up he raised his voice, 'Why are you here?' He repeated his demand three times, getting louder each time. We kept silent until he paused.

" 'We wish to thank you very much for the privilege of coming to see you,' I ventured.

"He said, 'Stop talking. Tell me what you want.'

"I whispered to Winston, 'You talk to him while I pray.' Finally the Prime Minister looked up, pointed to the chairs, and demanded, 'Sit down!'

"Abruptly he walked between us and shouted at his guards, 'Send in the Permanent Secretary, *now.*' In those few moments we prayed, 'God, we're in trouble. Please intervene. Send Gabriel, Your powerful Holy Spirit, whatever is needed to change his harsh attitude.' "

"Wow, what a reception!" Becky commented.

"When the Permanent Secretary came in, he looked at Winston and asked, 'What is your nationality?'

" 'I'm Guyanese.'

" 'And yours?' He looked at me.

"I said, 'I am from the United States.'

" 'What is your immigration status right now?' His demanding tone was the same as the Prime Minister's.

" 'I have been in Guyana now for nearly two years,' I said, 'on a one-year work permit, which has been renewed for a second year.' Then I turned to the Prime Minister and said, 'I suppose you know, sir, that we have been working with your wife on replacing a burned-down house in Arau, where the occupants lost everything.' When I said that, both men calmed down."

"God's Spirit and the angels must have been hard at work bringing peace into that room," Becky interjected.

"You're right, Becky. It was as if someone had turned on the light switch. He sat down, put his head in his hands, and sat there motionless for at least a minute. When he lifted up his head, he said, 'Gentlemen, I'm so glad you came today. I've heard much about your work. What can I do to serve you?'

"He wasn't the same man. Jesus answered our prayer. From that time on all four of us chatted about Guyana, the interior and its needs, and what type of TV broadcasting station would work for the area. They mentioned some technical concerns and showed interest as I shared some of our experiences working in Guyana. I felt as if four old friends had gotten together for a friendly chat."

"What a miracle of changed attitudes! Only God's presence could have driven away the evil angels. Did the Prime Minister talk much?" Becky asked.

"Yes, we laughed as he told jokes and anecdotes of his canoe trip up the Kamarang river to Waramadong and then to Paruima. I emphasized how we had been working closely with all the government agencies, and assured them that our medical evacuation service included everyone in need, that it made no difference what church they belonged to. All have equal access to medical care. We talked for at least forty-five minutes."

"Will they support this new TV station?" Becky asked.

"Yes, both of the men expressed confidence that permission and support would be granted. He promised to meet with his cabinet the next day. 'Tomorrow you should have your answer,' he said."

David continued, "Before we left I asked them if they would mind a word of prayer. They agreed. I asked God to bless them in their important responsibilities, and surround them with His presence and protection, giving them wisdom in their work. They seemed appreciative."

"David, that experience tells me that time must be very short. I think God wants us to move faster into other areas of Guyana."

"You're right. When we contacted the Frequency Management Unit (Guyanese equivalent of the FCC) the man said, 'The Prime Minister just called. We are to grant you the license for the TV station you requested.' He asked if we would be willing to build a second TV station at Lethem, a town near the Brazil border. Being the only religious TV stations in Guyana, this broadcast ministry will reach into thousands of homes."

"Truly God answers prayer," Becky said, looking heavenward.

"I must tell you more, Becky. As you know, God impressed our friend, Dan Peek, the electronics engineer, to volunteer to work with me on TV station installations. While working on getting two satellite dishes out of customs for the NET '98 series, he stopped by the Frequency Management Unit for some technical clarification he needed. He discovered they had already received instructions from the cabinet to proceed with granting us the station license."

"Amazing! Things seldom work that fast in Guyana."

"Listen to this. They've told us we will be able to use Channel 7. We wanted that channel because of its proximity to the commercial bands.

Lots cheaper, too. And we liked the significance of seven for the seventh-day Sabbath."

"Tell me about NET '98 that begins in October. Where will you put the two satellite dishes in Georgetown?"

"Dan is also coming down to help me install them. We will put one up at the Smyrna church where Winston attends, the other at the church in Linden. Both of these churches are preparing to be downlink sites for NET '98. Smyrna has prepared a large tent by the church to care for expected visitors. They've found many interested people through door-to-door visitation. I know God's Spirit will do great things in this area through NET '98 evangelism."

From that time on, David began a heavy flight schedule, providing medical and development support to the eight villages around Kaikan. Sad news came from Phillippi. During his absence eight people in that village had died from malaria. He transported new stocks of fuel and oil for the four chain saws being used to cut lumber for the second Paruima school building. He also saw lumber lying in neat piles waiting to be used as soon as construction could begin on the Kamarang TV station building.

But David faced a serious problem. He discovered he had only enough money to pay the woodcutters for their work in July. Where would he get enough to cover their wages for August and part of September? Surely God, who had intervened so often before, would provide sufficient funds. He prayed and waited. Nothing happened.

CHAPTER 20

A Call to Sacrifice

David urgently needed to make a trip to the United States. The date set for departure kept getting closer. Donations were nowhere close to the amount needed to break even. Taking his pen, he listed his debts. He needed $1,500 to pay August and September wages; $1,000 for aircraft fuel; $1,500 for roofing and construction materials for the TV station in Kamarang; and $1,000 to set up the second NET '98 satellite dish and receiver.

Once more he turned to his heavenly Financier. "God, I'm in trouble again. I have only $2,000 in cash, and I need at least $2,000 more. Even an additional $1,000 would resolve the immediate wages and materials problem. That would give me a few more days to pay the fuel and satellite receiver bill in town. This is Thursday morning. Friday is the last banking day, and my scheduled departure to the U.S. is Sunday night. I need Your help desperately. The extremity of the situation is Your great opportunity."

Knowing that God had previously provided emergency funds by putting cash in his briefcase, David confidently took the $2,000 and flew to Kaikan, two hundred miles deep into the jungle, where there are no banks and no possibility of getting several thousand more in cash. He had absolutely no doubt that once again God would supply the needed funds by placing an additional $2,000 in his briefcase while he slept.

Shortly after he landed in Kaikan, a miner approached him.

"Please take me to Georgetown. My wife is very sick, and I need to be with her."

"I'm sorry, but I do not plan to fly to Georgetown until Sunday. But I will take you to Kamarang tomorrow morning, where you can catch a commercial flight."

He rested well that night, with not a worry about the needed funds. The next morning, in high spirits, he began his devotions, thrilled once again at the story of Elijah and the widow. In his soul he praised the Lord for having met the need and for the extra $2,000 that he "knew" God had placed in his briefcase during the night.

After a prayer of thanksgiving and praise, the time came to count the evidence. Remembering the previous year when God miraculously converted $200 to $1,050, David confidently expected yesterday's $2,000 had been converted now to $4,000. He began counting, "$100, $200, $300, $400, $500; $1,000, $1,500, $2,000." He counted again, reaching only $2,000.

"How could You do this to me, God?" he asked. "You know I have only half of what we need this month to cover minimum expenses. How am I supposed to stretch $2,000 into $4,000?"

Upset and disappointed, David felt that God had let him down. In his exasperated state of mind he forgot the promise, "Our heavenly Father has a thousand ways to provide for us, of which we know nothing" (*The Desire of Ages,* p. 330).

Just as he had heard a year ago, David recognized that still, small voice whispering to him, *Use what you have.*

That's the problem. I don't have! he thought to himself with irritation.

Accustomed to conversing with God every day, he paused, knowing God had heard and would respond. While he waited, his eyes fell on the notebook computer on the bed beside him.

Didn't you get an offer to buy your computer last week for $2,000? the voice in his thoughts persisted.

David remembered that Pam Nickel, the newest volunteer teacher at the Paruima school, had arrived without a notebook computer. She had asked him to buy a similar one for her. They decided that she could have his computer the day he left. Then he'd replace his with a new one as soon as he arrived in the States. Pam agreed and gave him a check for $2,000.

Pam Nickel, a volunteer from Canada, teaches religion and English.

"But, God," David began to object, "You know that for the last fifteen years, as I've bought and sold notebook computers, I've carefully kept the money for replacement only. I'm unable to function without a computer. I use it for email, reports, digital images, Web page development, finance records, everything. How can I operate without a computer?"

Again David's mind registered the unwelcome thought, *Is God disagreeing with my assumption?*

In desperation he prayed aloud, "Now hold it right there, God. Surely You know the importance a computer holds in my work. You can't possibly imply that I should use my computer money for wages. I'd be crippled, completely lost without a computer. Unless You can clearly prove to me that this is what You want me to do, I cannot use those 'sacred funds' for anything other than the purchase of another computer."

Instantly the thought crossed his mind, *How can you expect others to sacrifice to send you funds, when you yourself are not willing to give until it hurts?* Was that the Holy Spirit speaking to him?

To add to his mental dilemma a whole string of Bible promises that he'd treasured through the years flashed through his mind in rapid succession. "Give, and it shall be given unto you ... pressed down, and shaken together, and running over ..." (Luke 6:38, KJV). "My God shall supply all your need according to his riches in glory by Christ Jesus" (Philippians 4:19, KJV). "He who calls you is faithful, who also will do it" (1 Thessalonians 5:24, NKJV). " 'But she out of her poverty put in all the livelihood that she had' " (Luke 21:4, NKJV). "For God loveth a cheerful giver" (2 Corinthians 9:7, KJV).

For a few moments the struggle in David's mind became intense. Then came the peace of surrender. Still on his knees, he submitted himself. "OK, God, I'm convinced. I'll use the computer funds to pay bills. It's exactly enough to meet the most urgent needs. I'll trust You for the purchase of another computer. If You want me to have one, You'll get me one somehow."

David felt like Abraham being asked to sacrifice his own son. His surrender played havoc with his emotions. Peace came with the decision, but a little depression set in at the thought of working and living without a computer.

Immediately he made plans to fly to the bank in Georgetown to cash the computer check. He sent word to the miner to come quickly to the runway. Overjoyed, the miner exclaimed, "Last night I prayed to God for the first time in a long time. I asked Him to somehow provide a way for me to get to Georgetown to comfort my wife. I'm amazed He answered so fast."

"That same God changed my mind this morning when I prayed, and sent me back to town even though I didn't want to go."

After landing in Georgetown, they prayed together at the airport, and David gave the miner a copy of Roger Morneau's book, *Incredible Answers to Prayer*. God had replaced David's feeling of loss with joy because his decision to obey had made him part of an answer to someone else's prayer. Maybe God would use his example to move other hearts to make similar sacrifices for God's work.

He cashed the check at the bank, picked up a few construction supplies, and hurried back to the airport. Two patients were waiting by the plane to go back to the interior. David loaded the plane with fuel, fastened in the passengers, and then remembered he hadn't checked his email.

Since he still had the notebook computer in his possession (he would deliver it to Pam on Sunday), he ran into the air taxi office, hooked up to the telephone line, and downloaded his email. Though he was in a hurry, he took the time to scan the subject lines of the eighteen messages that came in. One from his father entitled "Funds" caught his attention.

He read it quickly.

Son, your mother and I felt impressed by God last night regarding the urgency of the work being done in Guyana. We felt moved to give sacrificially to supply the needs of God's work there. We have written a check for $4,000, which will be deposited immediately in your Guyana account. Dad.

God had done it again! He had intervened to provide for His work. This time He hadn't put money in David's briefcase. Instead, God had done a greater miracle. He changed David's heart and moved the hearts of his parents to put "all on the altar of sacrifice." David knew they didn't have the spare cash any more than he had money to replace the computer. Now God had blessed both of them by entrusting them with the call to sacrifice. He knew they had both received joy from giving a real sacrifice, as he had in giving his computer. Somehow God's blessings make giving lead to receiving, which in turn leads to more giving. By working through His obedient children, God multiplies the resources.

As David walked back to the airplane, he praised God. "I feel most blessed. You trusted me enough to ask me to give what I most needed. Without a doubt, You will still provide what I need in Your own time and way. Someday You will give me the 'desires of my heart.' Thank You for the privilege of working completely by faith. May this simple act today encourage others around the world to also make a total commitment to give all to You. My precious Father, I love You and am certain that You are able, and will provide for Your own." Enthusiastic at how God had provided, David decided to immediately invest the full $4,000 in the school and doubled the amount of construction workers.

On arriving in the United States, David spent several days without a computer.

He felt lost, handicapped, naked, as if he were going through withdrawal. During that time he received an email on his father's computer from the Inter-American Division president, Pastor Israel Leito.

"I've collected some funds for you personally. I'd like to buy you a satellite cellular phone. I know you could use one."

Several days later the thought occurred to him, *Maybe the president might authorize me to buy something other than a cell phone.* He discovered that the president wasn't at his office but in Brazil attending Annual Council. So David sent this email:

"Appreciate so much your kind offer of a cellular phone. However, would you allow me to purchase a notebook computer instead?"

The answer: "My dear Friend and Inspiration, the money is yours. You can use it to purchase any piece of equipment you think is most needed."

This David gratefully did. God replaced his gift with a better, faster notebook computer than the one he had sold. He thought, *We never really sacrifice for God. He always gives us something better!*

Television Miracles

David clearly remembered the exact event in 1993 that triggered his interest in broadcasting. He was walking through the TV section in a Sears store in Chattanooga, Tennessee when suddenly he heard the familiar voice of Dr. Gordon Bietz, then senior pastor of Collegedale SDA Church. He was being interviewed on TV by David's close friend and schoolmate, Stephen Ruf. The subject dealt with the then ongoing government siege of David Koresh and the Branch Davidian compound in Waco, Texas. David had been listening to National Public Radio the day before when they erroneously aired misinformation linking the cult with the Church. Though the General Conference rapidly moved to correct that situation, David still remembered the helpless feeling he felt in the pit of his stomach. He could see how fast the general public could be prejudiced against a group of people through a misinformation campaign.

Now he watched, fascinated as Dr. Bietz clarified the misunderstanding. *God was able to use Stephen because of his current work responsibility at the TV station,* David mused.

Suddenly a life-changing thought seared deep into his mind. *The most effective way to deal with a crisis is to be prepared beforehand. It is too late to start once the crisis breaks.*

Lord, if You ever present me with an opportunity to put up a broadcasting network, I won't miss it, David determined in his heart.

Prompted by the Guyanese Prime Minister's support for the first TV station, David decided to seek permission to build one in Georgetown. The government's answer? A strong "No." He asked again several months later. Still the answer was "No." The reason remained the same: "We don't want that kind of TV station in this city."

Again David asked God for wisdom. The answer came again, *Use what you have.*

"I do have a set of NET '98 tapes. But using commercial TV costs money. Please show me the way to go."

Soon after, a woman in the U.S. called him on the phone. "Brother Gates, you're praying about some special need. God impressed me to call you."

He replied, "I seldom ever share the subject of my prayers, but if God impressed you, I'll tell you the specific request I'm asking God. We broadcast NET '98 on satellite in two churches with good response. Now I'm impressed God wants us to air it to all of the Georgetown area. Government officials have refused to allow us to operate our own TV station, so I'd like to put it on commercial TV."

"How much does that cost?"

"In Guyana television is pretty cheap. In Trinidad it would cost about $10,000, but here it is only $3,000."

"That's exactly what I have. I'll send you $3,000 tomorrow."

David quickly contacted Channel 13 and arranged for them to broadcast NET '98 three days a week for ten weeks beginning March 19, 1999. Since the series had already finished in the U.S., David emailed everyone asking for all the leftover Bibles, booklets, signs, envelopes, response cards, Bible studies, lesson outlines, and brochures. "Send them to my father in Anna, Illinois," he wrote, "and he'll forward them to Guyana." David received nearly a thousand pounds from all around the United States. Two pallets of materials cleared customs duty free. Working closely with the conference administration, all of the area churches received supplies.

Almost every church member joined in the preparations. A telephone hotline, staffed by a pastor's wife, answered callers' requests. Pastors and elders organized prayer teams and visitor welcoming teams. Young people distributed brochures to private homes and the public. Large newspaper advertisements ran in Sunday editions. Channel 13 aired advertising spots free throughout the ten weeks. God blessed the radio ads also, for they attracted many listeners. Requests poured in for free materials.

Baptist and Pentecostal pastors, people from all Christian denominations, even Hindus and Muslims, said they had found truths for which they'd been looking. People in government offices and banks, members of the upper class and well-educated people in the city called the hotline number for free books and Bible studies. Many asked, "Who's sponsoring this series? We like Dwight Nelson's style."

They heard the answer, "A group from the United States."

The Seventh-day Adventist churches in Georgetown stood ready when Pastor Nelson presented the topic of the Sabbath. They welcomed many visitors who accepted the invitation on TV to attend local churches. One Pentecostal pastor, deeply impressed with what he had learned, said, "I've been a pastor for years and never heard about the Sabbath." When he presented these Bible truths to his church, they requested a visiting Adventist evangelist, Brother Osmond Baptist, to present the Sabbath topic in person. The pastor and a large number of his congregation accepted the Sabbath truth.

NET '98 made a tremendous impact on Guyana. Many people called in to thank the TV manager for airing such high-quality programs.

Around this time David and Becky received an email from a close friend in the United States that shocked and hurt them. It was filled with criticism and accusations. Could the criticisms be true? Realizing that when God tries to reach people in trouble He often uses close friends, they chose to accept these criticisms as possibly true.

On their knees, with tears in their eyes, David and Becky confessed their weaknesses to God. David prayed, "Precious Father, You know some folk feel critical of the many projects that have opened up in this ministry. We're also amazed at the opportunities You have placed in our laps. This is Your mission, not ours. We open our hands and purposefully let go of all the projects so close to our hearts. We do not do this as an act of discouragement, but as an act in faith. We completely release to You all the work in Guyana."

"Yes, dear God," Becky said, joining the prayer, "we know You can reaffirm Your call to us. If not, we have faith that You can find someone else to do the job. In these two years You have amazed us by Your trustworthiness as we took larger and larger risks each month. We've discovered we cannot out-give You, God. The more we give to others, the more we receive from You."

David interjected, "We don't need to remind You, God, that in this year we regularly committed ourselves to monthly projects thirty to forty times bigger than our beginning budget of $200 a month two years ago. We have experienced the truth that 'the little that is wisely and economically used in the service of the Lord of heaven will increase in the very act of imparting' " (*The Desire of Ages,* p. 371).

Becky concluded her prayer with, "We praise You and thank You, Lord, that You are teaching us 'to impart of that which we have; and as we give, Christ will see that our lack is supplied' (*Testimonies for the Church,* vol. 6, p. 345). However, unless You clearly reveal otherwise, we will return home to the U.S. We make this painful decision because we do not want to rebel against Your will. Amen."

David and Becky felt the Holy Spirit calling them to a renewed commitment. Arm in arm on their knees, they pleaded that God would do something special to reaffirm their calling to Guyana.

That very same night a Seventh-day Adventist pastor named Kirk Thomas called David. "My landlord has asked to see you. He's the owner of Channel 2 television. His wife, Mrs. Washington, chose to be baptized partly as a result of NET '98. As a child she and her family had known the Adventist message but chose to leave it. She and her husband were favorably impressed with the way Dwight Nelson shared Bible truth and sent word they wanted to develop a relationship with you."

David, delighted at the invitation, hoped they wanted to offer him free time or perhaps a low-cost alternative for future broadcasts. Pastor Thomas arranged the visit for David to meet them two days later.

The Washington family welcomed Pastor Thomas and David to their beautiful home. As they sat together on the breezy porch drinking orange juice, Mr. Washington leaned forward.

"We appreciated what we saw on Channel 13. My wife recently became an Adventist. Someday I'll probably choose to join her. We built our TV station with spiritual purposes in mind. Only through God's intervention did we get this television station. Recently we've heard of your work with ADRA, what you are doing with aviation and medical work, and your involvement with education in the interior. Now we understand you have recently gotten into broadcasting. My wife and I have something special we'd like to present to you. We believe God wants us to give you 50 percent ownership of our TV station."

Speechless, David's mind raced over his yearlong failure to get a license to build a TV station in Georgetown. Had God been saying, "Wait on Me, David. When the time comes it's not difficult for Me to give you a fully operational TV station"?

Mr. Washington continued, "I want to turn over the complete administration of the TV station to you, to use as you see fit to carry forward your mission. I will remain involved enough to ensure that the station doesn't run into snags—legal, political, or otherwise. My goal is that this TV station must remain on the air and grow into its full potential."

Mr. and Mrs. Washington took the two men to the station. "You may use the complete two-story house and guest rooms as you see best, maybe as a studio or production center. What is your financial strategy to operate and expand the station?"

"Our philosophy is simple, Divine support. In all our operations we depend completely on God for operating and growth capital from month to month."

"I'm comfortable with that!" he stated emphatically. "Take the station and run with it."

David could hardly wait to share this marvelous news with Becky. "God has just worked another miracle. You remember our prayers two days ago. Well, He has not only reaffirmed His clear call to this ministry, but He's confirmed it by giving us a TV station."

"I don't understand. How could that be?"

"God impressed Mr. and Mrs. Washington to place a fully-operational TV broadcast station, including all assets, into our hands for finishing God's work here. Obviously, He intends to use the broadcast work big time to spread the gospel."

"But who will operate it?"

"This will demand a level of volunteer staff and resources far beyond anything we have experienced. Truly this is a God-sized task, for whose success only God can take credit. We must discard all preconceived limits of what He will do."

"Wow! I feel goose bumps all over me. Have you committed to accept this task regardless of how expensive or impossible it may seem?"

"Yes, Becky. We must learn by firsthand experience that the God we serve has *no limits*. We must move forward encouraged that He will provide during the difficult days ahead. Before their proposal becomes final, we will have several sessions with the Washingtons to discuss operating concerns and lay out strategic plans for operation and expansion."

"I fear that Satan is pretty mad about this, David. He'll do his utmost to prevent this station from being used by God. As Mr. and Mrs. Washington begin to understand our philosophy of depending on God for everything, I fear Satan will begin his warfare of doubt. We need prayer partners everywhere to ask God to circle the Washington family with light from heaven that will protect them from Satan's evil schemes."

No Limits

The good news of God's miracles of grace in Guyana spread from country to country in the Caribbean and South America. Requests from church leaders and members came pouring in. "Help us. Please show us how we begin to do what God is doing through you."

"Could it be that God is telling us the time has come to move ahead as though there were no limits?" David asked Becky.

"We must pray for wisdom. Maybe this is God's call telling us it's time to take a trip to the States. We can ask our parents to join us in Bible study and prayer for God's specific direction," she suggested.

Back in the United States, David laid the situation before their families. "Just as our small two-seater bush plane opened doors to influence the beginning of the ministry in western Guyana, so a faster, long-range plane will be needed to work through the Caribbean and South America."

For days they studied, prayed, and struggled with a large financial decision. This choice would seriously impact how they would work and risk in the future. Finally peace came. God impressed them to invest funds from the sale of a piece of the Gates farm in Illinois to partially finance the purchase of a small twin-engine aircraft. David's parents, always supportive, offered to sell a neighboring piece of land as well to put into the plane's acquisition. They needed a plane capable of safely and rapidly moving personnel and equipment between isolated regions and countries. David began hunting for the right plane God would choose.

He located a Piper Twin Comanche with a Robertson STOL kit and a special Miller cargo-nose conversion. To his amazement, he found the aircraft was the identical one he had flown many years before in Kentucky. Repeatedly during negotiations, the sale appeared to fall through. One time the family stopped everything and knelt in prayer. "God, You know the future. If this is not the plane that You have separated for our use, then allow the sale to collapse."

Within minutes the phone rang and the owner said, "I will accept your terms of purchase. You may come to inspect and test-fly the aircraft."

David, his father, and Brooks Payne, the director of maintenance for Andrews Aviation Airpark, flew to San Jose, California, to inspect the plane. Every item of concern they mentioned, the large aircraft facility immediately dealt with at their own expense.

The decision to purchase this plane implied a serious debt. "We're experiencing a similar decision as when we purchased our first small plane, but at a much higher level of risk," David explained to his father. "This plane requires 75-percent financing, a step we would never have taken were it not for the conviction and peace Becky and I, as well as you and Mom, share."

By faith they prayed again, "We believe this risk for needed equipment is Your will, God. We ask that You pay off the balance of the debt within six months of the date we take out the loan. You know the amount and what to do. Only You can provide the solution."

They flew the beautiful six-passenger aircraft to Michigan and loaded it with 550 pounds of broadcast equipment for the TV station in Kamarang. David flew it to Guyana with Dan Peek, who, with his wife, Cynthia, and small daughter, Hannah, would come as volunteers to Georgetown to head up the technical area of broadcasting.

Almost a month had gone by since their last visit with Mr. and Mrs. Washington.

After friendly greetings David began the discussion. "May I review the philosophy upon which we previously agreed? The operation of the TV station will not be based on commercial interests. We will trust God for finances."

By various comments they made, David soon realized that they had been reconsidering their willingness to accept such an arrangement. The enemy had been at work to bring their focus back to the world's philosophy—profit focused instead of mission driven. As David listened to them, he knew that they would expect him to pursue profitable programs that might conflict with the mission of the gospel. He could foresee problems arising from salary-driven employees, and rent that must be paid by volunteers.

"I'm sorry, but I feel that God would be displeased with that arrangement." David said and left the interview with a heavy heart. Only God could change attitudes and combat the unseen forces hard at work to prevent the station from being used for God's glory.

His constant prayer was, "My Father, everything depends on Your power and grace. Help the Washington family to perceive the heavenly philosophy that comes only from a vision of a God whom we can trust to provide."

David prepared a three-page document, laying out the faith philosophy under which he worked. He stated why all his previous proposals to pour funds into the project depended solely on pursuing the mission, not the profit. Then he called Mr. Washington asking for another appointment at 4:30 the next afternoon. All that day David and his friend, Winston, prayed together and individually asked God to intervene in behalf of His work. David also emailed his prayer partners regarding this crisis.

They met at the Washington home at peace, knowing God was still in charge. Yet they felt tense at the realization of how much hung in the balances. Truly they faced another episode in the great controversy between Christ and Satan.

While Mr. and Mrs. Washington read the three-page document, the two men continued in silent prayer. As he read, Mr. Washington underlined certain lines and nodded his head "yes" to each one.

When his wife had finished reading, she explained, "Last Thursday we invited Winston to our home to tell him why we had decided to maintain the TV station as a company for profit. Not only would it provide income for us, but also pay rent for volunteer staff that would stay there. But as Winston explained the history behind your faith operation, we sat amazed, listening to the story of God's miraculous leading.

"All day Friday I felt uncomfortable with the position we had taken. From my business I called my husband and told him my concern. Together we decided that God must be convicting us to withdraw our commercial interests in the station. He impressed us to step out and accept the faith philosophy of this operation. Frankly, we're a bit frightened by the idea of running a TV station totally by faith. However, we acknowledge that we also believe God will provide. We want to experience God's power in our lives."

Mr. Washington added, "We also decided you may have the use of the entire building rent free. You will pay only minimal costs for the upkeep. The TV station will operate with a totally mission-driven vision. I'm sure God won't have problems with the finances. We shall watch to see how He will provide for production. We trust He'll strengthen the station's signal and expand it by the use of repeaters to outlying towns."

David and Winston drove away singing songs of rejoicing. "Winston, the program is back on track with even more commitment than before. God intervened marvelously. Only His Spirit can change hearts and minds. Oh, the power of prayer! One more spiritual battle won for the Lord!"

Within a couple of weeks after the new plane's arrival in the Caribbean, David and Dan Peek flew to Grenada, Dominica, Antigua, and Tobago to meet with church leaders and government officials to set up plans for setting up Adventist TV broadcast stations. The growing TV network developed into what is known today as the Caribbean Family Network (CFN).

God faithfully provided sufficient funds to keep up the monthly payments on the new plane and pay the full balance. The small Cessna 150 that opened the work in Guyana was sold to pay half of the outstanding debt on the Twin Comanche.

Just before David made his second flight to Guyana with TV equipment, the left engine of the Twin Comanche developed a high engine oil temperature. He landed at the nearest airport in Tennessee, where he discovered that several engine push-rod tappets had begun wearing severely and had spread metal shavings through the engine.

He called Becky. "We've had a disappointing setback. The engine needs to be rebuilt. But that's balanced by the good news that the emergency happened in the U.S. at an excellent airport to get the work done. When it's finished it will be a much better engine than before. The right engine will also be checked for worn tappets before the plane is released for service. We see God in control, for He alone knows the future."

Back in the interior of Guyana, the Amerindian people in the Upper Mazaruni district continued to respond to the presentation of the gospel. The five video projectors kept running consecutive five-week village evangelistic efforts year round. In nearly two years of constant use and tropical transportation by canoe and on foot, only two projector bulbs had to be replaced. Three villages began construction of a church, and two others laid plans for their own church.

Guyana has nine regions, and the work with projectors and flight support are present in only one region—the Upper Mazaruni district. So what about the needs of the large, un-entered districts adjacent to them? Village captains came asking for a medical aviation program and Bible workers to conduct evangelist crusades. Without a support plane and professional pilot-mechanics and medical workers, the calls remained unanswered. Filled with sadness, David observed, "Most of my life I labored where opening new work was difficult and risky because of religious intolerance. Not so here. Will the opportunities open today soon disappear? Father God, grant the petitions of these villagers who want to know God."

The challenge of financing TV stations loomed much larger than that required by the plane. God clearly showed His power in enabling the building of one small TV station and the gift of a larger second one. Through them He provided opportunities to open work in two new countries. His providence made available a more reliable and efficient twin-engine aircraft to enter new regions. But with so many who still don't know God, who would come and help?

With absolute confidence David and his volunteers stood ready to cooperate with the blessings God would provide. They did not know what to do, but their eyes remained on Him.

All these developments that helped thousands of souls respond to Jesus, made Satan angry and desperate. Since his efforts to attack from the outside had failed, he tried to divide from within. Someone with experience and influence must have felt threatened with the growing success of this work, because at a meeting the person proposed that the Guyana Conference of Seventh-day Adventists terminate any relationship with David and Becky and their projects.

Every crisis becomes a call to fall on your knees before God. David and his family did just that. Union and division administrators quickly intervened, arranging another meeting with the purpose of restoring a strong working relationship. God, still in control, smoothed over the difficult spots. The group discussed and voted specific plans for better communication and coordination regarding each project. A time was arranged when the newly elected leaders would visit the developing projects in the interior. They could observe firsthand and ask questions to know each phase of God's work.

By the power of the Holy Spirit, eyes opened as the brethren realized that God's people aren't yet good enough, hot enough, daring enough, or filled with vision enough for this splendid hour of opportunity.

CHAPTER 23

The Lion Roars

Carrying evangelistic videotapes and professional equipment donated for the new TV station in Georgetown, David left the United States for Guyana. Flying just ahead of a winter cold front, he made overnight stops in Miami, Puerto Rico, Dominica, Grenada, and Trinidad, all the while keeping in contact by high-frequency radio with his father in Illinois. On the way, David constantly prayed that God would impress the Guyanese government to grant his organization, Guyana Adventist Medical Aviation Service (GAMAS), a permanent operating permit so that GAMAS airplanes could operate in Guyana without restrictions.

Upon his arrival David heard from Winston James. "God has been preparing the way for the arrival of the plane in Guyana. The Department of Civil Aviation had been preparing the paperwork. Many prayers continue to ascend for God's intervention."

Truly "when God opens the way for the accomplishment of a certain work and gives assurance of success, the chosen instrumentality must do all in his power to bring about the promised result. In proportion to the enthusiasm and perseverance with which the work is carried forward will be the success given. God can work miracles for His people only as they act their part with untiring energy" (*Prophets and Kings,* p. 263).

During David's absence from Guyana, the scheming enemy of God had been extremely active. The "father of lies" employs hostile people to undermine the work of God at every level of operation.

First, Satan chose someone who knew how to blacken David's character with insinuations. He accused David of manifesting criminal behavior and teaching heretical doctrines. Second, a newspaper article appeared, publishing these accusations. Third, the accuser visited the Washington family, owners of the TV station, to try to convince them to withdraw their support of the project because of David's bad reputation. The man expressed his opinion that he himself deserved to be given the station. God overruled, however, because the Washingtons became more convinced than ever that they had acted as the Holy Spirit directed.

The enemy planned to disrupt legal proceedings on the airplane and TV station, an insidious way to hinder God's work. But God, still in control, has His plans to proceed in spite of Satan. Knowing the power of prayer, David and his family and friends asked for special angels to ensure his safety as he continued his work for God. With heaven's blessings, David kept his schedule of three days of flying around the Guyana interior and a trip to the U.S. on a commercial airline.

Ugly rumors spread rapidly. When David checked in at the airport a special officer stayed by him, asked dozens of questions, and looked through his bags. After two hours of interrogation, he seemed impressed with the projects that God had begun in the interior under David's leadership. Since then David and the special officer have become close friends.

How did God quiet the roaring lion? As arranged before, David flew the church conference administration of Guyana to each of the villages in the Upper Mazaruni area. With their own ears, they heard the gratitude expressed by the captains from Arau, Kamarang, Phillippi, Kako, Waramadong, Paruima, and Kaikan. They saw the packed churches and heard of the lives saved by GAMAS as patients received free medical care and air transportation. They attended several church dedications and joined in the dedication of the religion and library building at Davis Indian Industrial College at Paruima. Still looking for ways to defame David, someone asked in a loud voice, "Who owns these churches and schools that have been built by donated money?"

A captain of one of the villages, a man of authority, gave a wise answer that stopped the rumor that David Gates owned them. "Whenever a building, be it a church or a school, is built for the Amerindians, the ownership never goes back to those who financed its erection. It belongs to the Indians. Therefore, according to the law of the land, all these churches and schools are the property of the Amerindians." The accusations stopped abruptly.

The visitors saw the results of the video projectors that had been taken to all the villages showing NET '95 and NET '98. They saw for themselves that more Indians had been baptized in three months of that year than the entire year before. The warm welcome and enthusiasm of the Amerindian people, showing spiritual growth, convicted them of God's leading and blessings. No human being could accomplish so much. The local and overseas volunteers received well-deserved praise for their dedicated service.

The conference visitors heard the village captains and community leaders throughout the regions strongly urge that the cabinet approve a permanent operating permit so that GAMAS would have the freedom to travel into every corner of Guyana without restrictions. Thus, the policy of free medical care and transport could be implemented throughout the country. No wonder Satan's anger became fierce. He well knew that granting the permit would open doors for the rapid spread of the gospel in Guyana's interior.

The visitors agreed with David, who concluded with the plea, "We must not hesitate to move forward. ' "Thus far the Lord has helped us" ' (1 Samuel 7:12, NKJV). If anything is accomplished for God's purposes it must be done at this golden moment."

David thanked God that for now, He had muffled the roar of the lion. But he recalled 1 Peter 5:8, which warned that David and the volunteer associates would no doubt hear the accuser's ugly roar again.

CHAPTER 24

Is Anything Too Hard for the Lord?

One Sabbath afternoon David and Becky enjoyed the rare opportunity to reminisce as they sat together on the porch of their Kaikan home.

"I feel so peaceful here, sitting with you, watching the river flow by," Becky said and squeezed David's hand. "I'm glad for Sabbaths when we can worship here in our little Kaikan church. The people's faces glowed as you played your trumpet with their singing. God has used your trusty trumpet to attract many visitors to the meetings.

"I feel blessed for this God-given privilege to serve Him among these precious people. Since we pledged to God that this year we would not turn away from any opportunity to reach people for Christ, He's certainly tested our commitment."

"Yes, He has. I marvel at God's plans, so much greater than we ever dreamed. Each day He reminds us that it is our duty to go forward, while it is His work to open the way. And look what He's done, Becky. Davis Indian Industrial College (D.I.I.C.) has been operating for almost three years, and also the successful Bible Worker Training School for adults. Do you remember the day God opened the way for the training school?"

"Tell me about it," she said.

"A thirty-five-year-old mother of eight children came to me and asked, 'May I come to your secondary school?' I felt sad telling her that we had no room for her. But she continued to plead, 'I always had a dream to go to school. Now we have one here. Please let me go to school and learn.'

"So God used her to spark the idea to invite older Adventist people to attend a day school for volunteer Bible workers."

Becky smiled. "But we had no competent volunteer teacher to lead them. Tell me again how God opened that door."

"Dear Dr. Sheila Robertson, a retired physician in her mid-seventies, arrived as a volunteer with this request: 'Please take me to the most isolated village

Dr. Sheila Robertson with Ada and Sebastian Edmund

where I can serve God.' I flew her in twenty minutes to Phillippi, a distance that would take four or five days to walk, and instructed her, 'Here's a little radio to keep in touch every day, more often if you need it.' I left her there, and she loved every minute, doing a marvelous work for God. One day when I flew in to Phillippi for a short visit with her, she shared with me her idea of opening a Bible Worker Training School for adults and older young Amerindians. Because they speak the local dialects of Akawayo and Arecuna and are Amerindians themselves, they don't need government permission to enter the villages. I admitted that I too had been dreaming about the same thing, but didn't have anyone to direct the program."

" 'I like working in remote, isolated areas best,' she told me. 'Paruima is a large village of about six hundred. But if God needs me to head it up, I will not say no.' "

"I remember the enthusiasm radiating from the faces of those nine Amerindian Bible workers at their graduation," Becky added. "Going out two by two under the tutoring of experienced conference Bible workers, seven have already begun pioneer mission work in unentered areas. God has surely worked through Dr. Sheila."

"Without volunteers our work here would be impossible. As team leaders and directors, they keep each area moving forward. I'm sure God will answer our prayers for at least fifteen long-term volunteers, mostly teachers, this year. But the short-term volunteers add great blessings too."

"Yes, David," Becky said with a smile, "what a thrill to see the academy kids and their principal from Dakota Adventist Academy fit in. Only the angels know how hard they worked as they prayed and played with the kids and adults in the villages. I wonder how many shuttles it took to move half the group between Kaikan and Arau with the Cessna 206.

"The large group from Laurelbrook Academy made a lot of progress on building the new school at Kimbia on the Berbice River."

"Becky, you should have seen how the presence of Pastor Phillip Follett, a general vice-president of the General Conference of Seventh-day Adventists, encouraged the Amerindians as he led out in the dedication of the new video production studio at the Davis Indian Industrial College. Soon we hope to begin producing videos in dialect for education and evangelistic use throughout the region. I thrilled at how happy the Indians appeared at the groundbreaking for the new health science building at D.I.I.C., and at the dedication of the community TV station at Kamarang. Though it's not transmitting yet, the station is built and ready for action.

"Yes, Sweetie-pie, there's no limit to what God can do. When I think of those new Bible workers like Sylvester Robertson and his colleague, James Edwin, entering Isseneru village, I rejoice that those two hundred villagers have accepted them, and willingly listen to the gospel of the three angels' messages. In fact, Sylvester told me the other day that he is studying the Bible every week with the local Anglican priest, who appears to be accepting many of the truths. Sebastian Edmund and Ray Hastings opened up the work in Koopenang, where villagers provided for their needs as the Word of God was opened to them. With the graduation every six months of a new batch of Bible workers, several unentered villages are receiving the good news. Great things have happened since God impressed us with the philosophy that He could handle the finances. Our only fundraising would be through prayer to Him."

"Now, David, you know how I feel about your working so hard, but I know God foresaw the need that you become part of the conference team as director of ADRA Guyana, not as a paid conference employee but as a volunteer. I'm sure that part of the success of the work rests on the confidence and close working relationship with local church administrators. With your assistant director working at the Georgetown ADRA office, you've been free to join with leaders in six new countries this year.

"How true is the promise that 'if the work be of God, He Himself will provide the means for its accomplishment' " (*The Desire of Ages,* p. 371).

A few days later, when David flew to Georgetown, he heard of a local Cessna 172 for sale. It was the first single-engine aircraft that had been offered for sale since he had moved to Guyana. He determined not to miss this crucial opportunity of owning a locally registered plane. At the airport the director of maintenance rushed to him and said, "If you are thinking of purchasing the Cessna 172 that's for sale, you must move quickly. Already two others have met with the owner and CEO of the air taxi company offering to buy it."

"Thanks for warning me," David called as he ran across the airport ramp. He prayed aloud, "Lord, please don't let that locally registered aircraft be sold to someone else. You know about the unreached villages that have been patiently waiting for so many years." As he ran, he felt grateful that he had recently talked with a friend in the United States who had told him he would be putting a sizable gift into David's bank account in the U.S. to be used as a slush fund when needed.

He called the air taxi CEO on the phone.

"That's right, Captain Gates," the man affirmed. "Two others have made offers on the plane. I'll give you an appointment for 4:00 P.M. First come, first served, is my policy." And the CEO hung up.

David looked at his watch. He had thirty minutes to get to the bank before closing time. As he ran outside to find a taxi, the words from his morning devotions gave him his instructions: "The cause of God demands men who can see quickly and act instantaneously at the right time and with power" (*Gospel Workers,* p. 133).

After fifteen minutes he found a taxi driver willing to take him half way. On the way he prayed that another would get him there in time. He planned to arrive at the CEO's office with the down payment in his pocket.

Still talking to God, he prayed, "Lord, You have blessed me with financial credibility everywhere I've worked. I know the tellers by name. You know that getting funds transferred through foreign banks can be a lengthy process. Only You can impress the teller to react favorably when I try to cash this large foreign check. Thanks for handling this with speed."

As he walked up to the bank counter, a friendly teller smiled. "Good afternoon, Mr. Gates, what can I do for you?"

"Could you please cash this personal check right away. I have an important appointment."

She looked at it briefly. "I'll get the necessary signatures from the administration and be right back with the cash." In just a few minutes she handed him US$10,000 in cash!

"Thank you so much," David said, smiling, and hurried to find another taxi. Back at the airport he spoke quietly to a friend, the air taxi company's chief pilot. "I'm coming to this appointment with the down payment in my pocket. I'm hoping to offer $5,000 less than the asking price."

However, with two other interested purchasers, he knew he had no negotiating power to offer less. Immediately the chief pilot got the CEO on the phone. "Mr. Gates is here with the down payment. You know this plane will be valuable in the medical work in the interior. Many Amerindians are alive because of his medical evacuation service. I recommend that you accept his lower offer."

"Tell Mr. Gates to come in for an interview," the CEO responded.

David stepped into the CEO's office. "Sir, Guyana's interior people need another airplane to serve their needs. Here is the down payment for the Cessna 172." David laid the cash on his desk, and continued. "I was planning on offering you $5,000 less than the asking price, but with two others also interested in the plane I know that—"

"I accept your offer, Mr. Gates," the CEO interrupted. "I will give orders right away for the bill of sale to be drawn up. You may wire me with the remaining balance tomorrow. I congratulate you for your prompt action. Had you waited until tomorrow, you probably would have lost the aircraft."

The CEO held out his hand and grasped David's. "Thank you so much, sir, for your consideration," David said. "I assure you I work under the direction of my heavenly Father who is really in control of GAMAS." David smiled his appreciation.

The CEO replied, "I have been most interested in the work you are doing in Guyana these last four years. You have been quick to jump at opportunities as they opened to the advantage of the Amerindians. I am convicted that this sale certainly is the best choice for the well-being of Guyana. As long as you help the Guyanese, even if they are Amerindians, I'm on your side."

As David left the CEO's office, he stopped in a secluded place to discuss the whole situation with his Divine Financier. "God, You know that the down payment as well as the rest of the funds will require 100 percent financing, something I am not comfortable with. I asked my long-time friend for ninety days when borrowing the funds to purchase that plane. I know I can never make that payment without direct Divine intervention. But I believe my duty is to go forward. Since that plane is vital to the advancement of Your work, I can rest in Your loving leadership and trust You with the finances. Thank You for opening the way and giving me the privilege of being a partner with You in this small section of Your vast universe."

The following morning David began a heavy weeklong flying schedule with the new Cessna 172. He moved fuel and supplies to the student missionaries. He dropped off the Amerindian Bible worker volunteers to begin their gospel work at their villages. The Cessna 172 carried several sick people to the hospital and even brought the body of a woman who had died in Georgetown for burial at her home village of Kamarang.

Peace and joy flooded his mind as he flew over those vast jungles. Buoyed up by the words from his devotions, God filled him with courage.

"You will have obstacles and difficulties to encounter at every turn, and you must with firm purpose decide to conquer them, or they will conquer you…. And if anything is accomplished to the purpose, it must be done at the golden moment. The slightest inclination of the weight in the balance should be seen, and should determine the matter at once" (*Gospel Workers*, p. 133, 134).

Certain that he had acted in accordance with this instruction, he now waited with excited expectancy to see God's response. David knew long delays tire the angels. Surely God's timing would not take long.

Less than ten days later, he received information from a donor that sufficient funds had been committed to repay the loan and make an additional deposit toward a new plane for Venezuela.

Why was Venezuela chosen? Christian young people had sprung into action distributing ADRA relief materials because of the disastrous mudslides in Caracas in 1999, which killed tens of thousands. Government officials had observed the honesty and caring of these Christian youth. Now doors had been opened and communities in need were asking for help from Seventh-day Adventists.

Venezuelan church leaders sent word to David, "Please join us as we meet with thirty village captains to discuss ways of reaching their isolated communities with medical care. The Amerindians in Guyana have shared the blessings they've received from the Guyana Adventist Medical Aviation Service with their friends across the river. These indigenous leaders have asked us here in Venezuela to establish a similar service among their people. With so much support from these captains for the project, we need your help and advice."

"I'll be glad to join you in any way I can," David replied. "If God is opening another door to reach the Amerindians, we must go forward under His direction."

David met with the ADRA directors for Canada, the Inter-American Division, and the Caribbean Union and guided them in preparing for the acquisition of an aircraft for Venezuela. He also stressed the need for volunteer leaders. All through the negotiations he thought, *How precious that God chose to use little Guyana to help its larger neighbor, Venezuela.*

When he returned to Guyana, David, bubbling with joy, longed to share all this with Becky. Using the HF radio he contacted her. "God Himself has begun to provide for the eternal welfare of both Guyana and Venezuela. I wish you had been there to experience the enthusiasm for volunteer service at the Adventist University in Nirgua. The Union is now working on a plan whereby all university graduates will be invited to donate their first year after graduation to volunteer for Church mission service. What would happen if that idea would infect all our college campuses worldwide?"

"Listen to this, Sweetie-pie," Becky responded. "Nothing says it clearer than the words of Moses. 'God is not a man, that he should lie; neither the son of man, that he should repent: hath he said, and shall he not do it? or hath he spoken, and shall he not make it good?' That's Numbers 23, verse 19" (KJV).

God Does It Again

The year 2001 brought new challenges that some would call enormous problems. From habit the volunteers in Guyana turned to God, for they knew His solutions would be miracles. They believed that God controls every facet of His work with the promise "to give you a future and a hope" (Jeremiah 29:11, NKJV).

The first challenge came as Dan Peek struggled alone to meet the large technical needs of building a transmitter to bring the station up to full power. He was also handling radio communication and station management. Though Dan did not complain, David started praying for a young Caribbean professional who could carry the station management. This would strengthen the local flavor of administration while freeing up Dan to focus on technical needs.

God's response was soon in coming. Esther Cedeno, a former student of David's at Caribbean Union College in Trinidad, responded. Holding a graduate degree in business management from Andrews University, she had already served for nearly a year in the village of Arau as a missionary teacher before returning home to Trinidad. Aware of the need in Georgetown, she told David that she had clearly seen God leading her to come back and serve as manager. Her tact and skills quickly earned her the respect and support of the entire team. Esther received management support through Jacqui and Peter Adams, who were directing the TV project in Trinidad and Tobago. Always willing to assist, Jacqui made several trips to Guyana and provided temporary administration when Esther was absent. God had answered once again.

Neither David nor Dan knew that God had a volunteer ready to solve a new crisis at the Davis Indian Industrial School (D.I.I.C.) in Paruima. One Friday morning, David dropped off a retired pastor and his wife, who was a librarian, at the airstrip. These older volunteers had come to organize D.I.I.C.'s first library, and also teach the Bible workers and conduct a Week of Prayer. That Friday afternoon, shortly before sundown, someone discovered that the spring, the water source for the area from Rain Mountain since the 1950s, had stopped flowing. River water would have to be used for cooking, drinking, and baths.

David Hosick pipes water to every building on campus.

But God had foreseen this problem. He prompted David Hosick, an ADRA volunteer engineer from Ontario, Canada, to offer his skills to D.I.I.C. from January to March 2001. Early on the Sunday morning after the water flow ceased, Hosick hiked half a mile up a steep trail to a large rock, the primary source of the spring. He discovered that mud and debris had filled the collection tank and clogged the water pipe that flowed down the mountain to the school. With student help they cleaned out the plastic collection tank, lifted it out, and excavated an area two feet down so that they could lower the tank. Then they built a concrete buffer dam. To prevent the water from becoming stagnant, he located the overflow pipe in such a way that the tank would always contain about eighteen inches of water.

Hosick realized that in dry years the spring would not be enough for a growing school. An older villager told him, "I can take you 400 feet above this spring to another source with a small waterfall coming from under a huge rock."

Thrilled at the possibilities, Hosick, with the help of students, carried cement up the mountain and built a concrete catchment basin below the waterfall. They covered the basin with metal sheets to keep out debris and small animals and attached a three-quarter-inch black plastic pipe. Slashing out heavy jungle growth, they created a fifty-foot drop almost straight down to the primary source. Water from both sources now flowed through a two-inch plastic pipe to a 1,000-gallon cistern at the foot of the mountain. Previously, this cistern had never been full in the history of the school, but now, with the increase of volume and pressure, it filled and overflowed in about five hours. The students dug ditches to direct the overflow to the school gardens. With the added flow, every building on the campus would have pure water piped to it. Jesus, the Water of Life, provided abundantly for His children.

Praising God for these miracle gifts from heaven, David had to turn his attention to another very important document. For the first two years he had been operating GAMAS airplanes on temporary permits. Then came the ultimatum, "No more temporary permits. Your planes are grounded until the government grants you a permanent permit." The only way David could fly into the interior was to rent a Cessna 206 at about $250 an hour or a twin Islander for $350 an hour. Each supply trip to the interior cost between $850 and $1,200.

Sharing his concern with his good friend Winston James, David explained, "GAMAS desperately needs permission from the Guyana government to officially operate a permanent aviation program in the country."

"You know that recent visits by the Prime Minister to Paruima and the country's president to Kamarang, have placed our permit application in the forefront," Winston responded. "Didn't you request an appointment with President Jagdeo?"

"Yes, we did. Along with the conference administration, we met with him on Monday, October 2, 2000, at 4:00 P.M. We prepared a master plan to 'storm' heaven with our pleas. Every church throughout the interior pledged to hold special prayer and fasting sessions. At 4:00 P.M. they rang the church bells, so every villager could stop what he or she was doing and pray for God's presence during that appointment."

"Wonderful!" Winston replied. "We know ' " 'that the Most High is sovereign over the kingdoms of men' " ' (Daniel 4:17, NIV). God heard those prayers. Tell me about the interview."

"We prepared a full written report of the past four years in color to present to President Jagdeo and his influential head of personnel, Dr. Loncheon. We gave a beautiful copy of Ben Carson's story, *Gifted Hands,* to the president's wife, who works closely with us in the medical care of children in the interior. The churches in Georgetown also prayed for God's presence and power. All our eyes looked to our Lord. We clearly felt God's presence during the interview, for His Spirit helped us to answer each question. After the president looked through the report, he stated, 'I am convinced this service is a great benefit to the many isolated villages in the interior. We will immediately begin processing the approval for GAMAS to receive permission to operate its medical aviation program throughout the country.'

"Leaving that interview, we truly felt that 'the One who calls you is faithful, and He will do it.' "

"But, David," Winston interrupted, "that interview happened last October. Both of your airplanes still sit at the airport. What happened?"

"Satan pulled out all his sly methods to counteract or delay what the president stated. Bureaucracy cooperated with Satan's schemes, requiring the clearance of numerous government agencies and ministries. First, they said they could not grant the permit until they had military clearance. Since we have benefited and worked with the military many times, that was approved without much delay. Word came from the ministry that in a short time we'd get the permit.

"Second, someone complained that the wording on the bill of sale on the Cessna 172 needed clarification. Immediately we went to work and had everything changed to satisfy them within twenty-four hours. Weeks went by. Still they delayed, so we called again.

"The third objection was, 'You need to clarify the supporting relationship of GAMAS to the Seventh-day Adventist Church.' We reminded them that the document had been written and was in their file. After more delays, they found it and appeared satisfied.

" 'Come back in two days and your permit will be ready,' they promised. But we waited, not knowing what new roadblock Satan would throw up in this delay game. The last word we received was that the approval paperwork had been completed, and the complete package would go to the cabinet for approval. Now the hold-up is that the Cessna 172 must be reregistered, a new certificate issued in GAMAS's name and the plane's air-worthiness certificate reissued. Thanks be to God, we see slow but steady progress."

With national elections coming up in the middle of March, David knew time was short. Hundreds of villagers fasted and prayed. With the expiration of the temporary operating permits, the small red airplane still sat on the ground awaiting final approval.

Just eleven days before the elections, David began to despair. But then God spoke to him in his morning devotions from Matthew 14:24, 25. "But the ship was now in the midst of the sea, tossed with waves: for the wind was contrary. And *in the fourth watch of the night Jesus went unto them,* walking on the sea" (KJV, italics supplied). Peace filled David's heart. He felt convinced that God was telling him that the permit would be issued at the last possible moment.

On Thursday morning, March 8, 2001, the Director of Civil Aviation (DCA) welcomed David with a smile. "The cabinet has given GAMAS full approval to operate in Guyana. Your patience and insistence during the last five years have paid off. Here is your permission to fly anywhere in Guyana."

The next Sabbath David flew in the little red airplane and landed at the airstrips of Paruima and then Kaikan. Jubilant village children and adults formed two circles around the Cessna 172 for a celebration of praise, prayer, and singing. Brimming with joy, David expressed his thanks to his praying Davis Indian friends.

"Even though we seemed to be struggling against apparently insurmountable difficulties, you continued to plead with God, expecting large things through faith in His promises. I'm sure we pleased God when we made the highest demands upon Him that we might glorify His name. For over five months Satan's hassles and delays kept our airplanes from errands of mercy in Guyana. Yet we know that God still controls the affairs of men. Though we cannot now understand why the long delay, we praise God that during the long wait, He gave us grace to keep our eyes fixed on Him."

During the next three days, before the Gates family was to take a trip to the United States, David kept the plane constantly in the air. He flew supplies to volunteers, picked up medical patients, transported visitors, flew in medications, and accelerated construction with the delivery of new chain saws and fuel to regions 7 and 8 of Guyana. Sensitive to the desperate need for pastoral support, a conference minister volunteered to be flown into the interior for two days by GAMAS. Between Paruima and Kaikan, he ordained elders and performed eight weddings. Four different baptismal events had to be scheduled as twenty-five people, hearing that a pastor was in the district, walked to Kaikan requesting baptism. The church members rejoiced that GAMAS planes could continue to bring hope, joy, and blessings into the interior.

Some time later, Dan Peek pulled David aside to discuss some technical matters, revealing a serious new complication.

"When Mr. and Mrs. Washington donated Channel 2, one of their requests was that we bring it to full power. The transmitter amplifier has been built, but it is not working properly. Frankly, I can't find the problem. If we can't get ours to work soon, we might have to consider purchasing a $30,000 transmitter."

Suddenly Dan remembered a friend who was very sharp in broadcast electronics and decided to contact him. Available for a few weeks, the friend came down and worked very hard on the equipment. It seemed apparent that very soon the station would be at full power. The friend made a trip to the U.S. for parts and returned to complete the job. After testing the modified amplifier, he provided David with a list of needs, including the recommendation to acquire a new transmitter. They were back to point zero.

Eighteen months after assuming control of the station, they were still transmitting at low power. At this time Dan and his family decided to return home to the U.S. where Dan hoped to pick up additional engineering experience in broadcasting. Expectations had been high, and credibility was running low. The crisis demanded a Divine solution.

First individually, then as a group, David shared his concerns with the station's board members. "I don't mind asking God to provide miracle resources to purchase the new transmitter. However, I feel convicted that while we have focused on the technical side of broadcasting, we have failed God in some areas of our programming.

"Everything we air must honor Christ and reflect our clear identity." Solemnly the board knelt to confess this weakness and to ask God's special blessing on the new change in direction.

With that commitment, both sides of the great controversy immediately mobilized for action. During the following two days while David was out of the country, outside forces attempted to wrest the TV station out of the board's control. Using inside financial information these individuals argued that only in a takeover would sufficient funds become available to buy the needed expensive new transmitter. Through apparent coincidences, David was able to keep one step ahead of each crisis.

With his heart full of joy at seeing God's hand in control and at peace over the direction the board had set, David confidently asked the Lord for the funds to purchase the urgently needed transmitter. Within twenty-four hours, a semi-retired couple contacted David, offering their retirement funds to purchase the equipment. God's promise kept ringing in David's ears, "And it shall come to pass, that before they call, I will answer; and while they are yet speaking, I will hear" (Isaiah 65:24, KJV).

Returning quickly to Guyana, David began overseeing the station's daily operations himself. Clearly, God's provision of the new transmitter had helped to restore confidence and credibility in the mission of the station. With Mr. Washington's help, technicians were contracted to install new satellite downlinks to 3ABN and AGCN, soon to include Safe TV. In harmony with the evangelistic mission of the TV station, David began developing a team of Bible workers to work with the distribution of literature and Bible studies offered by the station. Things were back on track again at TV2.

Some months before, David had confessed to Becky, "Have you considered that when we receive our permanent operating permit for GAMAS, we face another challenge. With God's added blessings come added responsibilities. I'm already spreading myself too thin. Without pilots and other mature people with leadership qualities, who choose to commit themselves on a long-term basis, progress in Guyana's interior will be stymied."

"You're right, David, but think of the volunteers God has sent. What would you have done without Dan Peek and his family, who as volunteers in Georgetown had handled all the technical TV situations; and faithful Dr. Sheila, who carries the leadership at D.I.I.C. in Paruima?"

David interrupted her. "Don't forget the excellent work of local volunteers as they teach in the village schools. D.I.I.C. could not continue without the student missionaries from Southern Adventist University in Tennessee, who teach all the classes. Joining them come volunteers from other countries—Canada, Germany, France, Slovakia, Trinidad and Tobago, Bolivia, and the state of Oregon, a total of fourteen volunteers for the school year. What wonderful dedication they have shown! We also have a great team of airplane mechanics in Georgetown. But now we need dedicated bush pilots, who feel committed to sacrifice the conveniences of time, home, family, and country to join the GAMAS team.

"I'm going to take our problem to the Lord. I shall ask Him to choose volunteers who will allow Him to make difficulties into challenges and delays into a time to develop trust and patience. He will impress people who will submit themselves to God, so that even in their failures, by God's power, they become victories to His glory." With that, Becky took her Bible and went to her bedroom.

Sometime later she ran down the stairs, threw her arms around David, and exclaimed, "God gave me the answer. Remember when Moses felt burdened with too much administrative work, and the Lord told him to gather seventy men? God said, 'I will take of the spirit which is upon thee, and will put it upon them; and they shall bear the burden of the people with thee, that thou bear it not thyself alone.' That's from Numbers 11:17 (KJV). I'm sure God at this very moment is preparing dedicated pilots who will step forward and volunteer to assist with the heavy flying loads."

Encouraged by Becky's confidence, they knelt and laid their burden on the Lord.

A few weeks later David and Becky headed for Southern Adventist University, where he had been scheduled to speak at alumni weekend. What he didn't know was that Southern had just elected him Alumnus of the Year as well. Scheduled as a keynote speaker for the collegiate church, David noticed that the gym was also full of middle-age and retired people. There were no empty seats. Somewhere out in the crowd, Orville Donesky and Gary Roberts, two pilots, felt impressed by what they heard David say in his sermon.

Gary had been raised in a medical missionary aviation family. Now a registered nurse, professional pilot, and mechanic, he'd been praying for God to lead him to a mission aviation program focused on medical work. The Holy Spirit spoke to his mind, *GAMAS is the answer to your search.* He was dating a girl who was also a registered nurse. He shared with her that he felt called to pioneer in an unentered region of Guyana's interior.

David had flown with Orville Donesky's brother, Conroy, in Mexico thirteen years before. Orville and his wife, Odil, with their children, seven-year-old Andrew and Kristena, age three, also felt God's Spirit encouraging them to consider joining the aviation work in Guyana. This would mean selling their lovely home and Orville resigning his lucrative research job as a mechanical engineer at McKee Baking Company in

Orville and Odil, Andrew and Kristena Donesky, with Gary Roberts

Collegedale, Tennessee. Though scared to venture out on such a drastic change of lifestyle, they began moving forward by faith.

Both Gary and Orville, along with Orville's family, felt such a strong commitment that they paid their own way to spend much of February 2001 in Guyana, flying with David. Having accepted an invitation from Clyde Peters at the airbase in Pucallpa, Peru, they took an intensive training course in jungle survival. Orville and Gary took turns copiloting the twin Comanche for an all-night flight across Brazil. They landed in Bolivia for a few hours' rest and refueling. When they arrived in Pucallpa, Peru that evening, they had no idea how God would open another door for the aviation ministry in Guyana.

The Peru Project's pilot, Alberto Marin, met them and said, "Come and look at the 'J. J. Aiken,' our first Cessna 182 bush plane. It's being rebuilt after some gear damage and will be stronger than new. We're now flying a second plane and praying for an interested buyer who will use the 'J. J. Aiken' to God's honor and glory."

Orville whispered to David, "Surely he can't know Odil and I are looking for a Cessna 182 to buy for Guyana?"

David shook his head. "There's no way he would know," he whispered back. "Could God have something special up His sleeve?"

Within days the price had been set, the sale approved, and all parties were excited that the plane would continue in God's work in Guyana. Half of the funds were paid, with the second half due in a few months, after the delivery of the plane.

Orville and Gary committed themselves to joining the GAMAS team of volunteers in the summer of 2001. David and Becky talked to them just before they boarded the plane to return to the United States. Orville, with his arm around Odil, opened his heart. "We cannot doubt God's promise in Isaiah 30:21, 'Thine ears shall hear a word behind thee, saying, This is the way, walk ye in it, when ye turn to the right hand, and when ye turn to the left' (KJV). God's peace floods our minds as we are reminded of God's promises to provide for all our needs. With trembling knees we've made plans to build a humble house on the banks of the Kamarang river near D.I.I.C. in Paruima, trusting God's hand to guide us. We are privileged to be part of the aviation program and to help share the administrative responsibilities at D.I.I.C. Someday soon everyone will need to trust God totally for everything. We have chosen to begin learning now and are overjoyed for opportunities to share what God has done for us."

Gary nodded his approval. "My visit to Guyana has affirmed my conviction that God is calling me to uphold this rapidly growing work in Guyana. I've made my decision too. Orville will be flying the new Cessna 182 to uphold the established work in Region 7, while I'll fly our current Cessna 172 with a new STOL kit to pioneer the work in Region 8. Together we're committed to the philosophy of divine support.

"At the same time we'll be loyal to God's church and message, working with the brethren. I'm excited at the possibility of joining God's people, working in unity to make a significant contribution toward the saving of precious Indians that now know nothing of God's power and grace."

Soon after, David received word from Warren McDaniel II, who had accompanied the Laurelbrook Academy group to work on the new school in Kimbia on the Berbice River. Warren and his wife, Jodi, along with their nine-year old daughter, Taylor, and their six-year old son, Warren III, had made a commitment to head up the new school, Berbice Adventist Academy, in Kimbia.

David squeezed Becky's hand and whispered, "What has encouraged me so much has been to witness Orville Donesky and Warren McDaniel both turn their back on very lucrative, senior management positions in big companies in order to follow God, along with their families, into the unknown as volunteers. Becoming a full-time professional missionary volunteer is kind of like being burned at the stake. Fascinated by radical sacrifice, people come to watch. As they do, they can see God's joy written all over the faces of the 'victims' and become infected with a desire to experience the same."

Too full of joy to speak, Becky wiped away the tears running down her cheeks.

David continued, "With a good team in Guyana, I have also been able to turn my attention to the growing needs of the Caribbean Family Network throughout the islands. Oh, I forgot to tell you that our good friend and long-time denominational co-worker from St. Lucia, Gilbert Jn-Francois, has joined our CFN team as the secretary of the corporation. God kept His promise to us. He provided the help we desperately need. We are only instruments in God's hands, willing volunteers for the Master's service, trusting God to make us all a blessing."

Bowing his head reverently, David prayed aloud, "Please, dear Father, our eyes are on You. Only You, who alone can read hearts and motives, can continue to impress committed workers to volunteer. You know of hearts that will be willing to sacrifice the conveniences of this life, yes, even life itself, to go 'to places where the very name of Christ has not been heard' (Romans 15:20, NEB). I rejoice over Your miracles of grace with airplanes, TV stations, schools, and medical-evangelistic work. These precious Amerindians are Your children, just as much as the millions that are reached by TV in the city. Thank You for the assurance that You will finish what You began. Like Joshua we lean on Your promise, 'Be strong and of a good courage; be not afraid, neither be thou dismayed: for the Lord thy God is with thee withersoever thou goest' (Joshua 1:9, KJV) We praise Your holy name. Amen."

A Conversation With David Gates

Q. David, what does it take to be a missionary?

A. The most necessary ingredient for successful mission service is an intimate relationship with God, accompanied by the conviction that God is leading you into mission service. When difficulties arise in one's work, I think it is essential to have that "sense of calling," which leads one to cast one's cares upon Him, who called you into His service, and ask Him to solve the problem. Some persons feel that sense of calling from youth, while others are impressed with it during a life experience or while visiting a foreign field.

Q. Does it require a certain personality or particular skills?

A. Every person is born with a different combination of interests, aptitudes, temperaments, and personalities. These become the raw materials to be improved and built upon through self-discipline and education. God has a place for every ability, talent, skill, and personality in His work. An understanding and acceptance of this principle is vital to being able to accept others and work with them as a team.

As taught by the miracle of the five loaves and two fishes in Matthew 14 and Mark 6, we are to recognize that we have a direct order from the Lord, "Give ye them to eat" (Mattthew 14:16, KJV). We should do an inventory of what we possess and place 100 percent in God's hands. He will then take what we give Him and multiply it sufficiently to carry forward His commands. Clear teaching on the use of our talents in Matthew 25 also reinforces this principle. Use them or lose them.

Suppose Japan and its culture fascinates you. On the assumption that your interests are a gift from the Lord and should be developed, you thank the Lord for this interest and submit your will to Him and ask Him to intervene at any time should He have another plan for you. But remember, obstacles are not necessarily evidence of God's disapproval. They are to be overcome. Meanwhile, you begin to read all about the culture and start to learn Japanese. You might plan a short mission trip to that country or serve there as a volunteer for a year. As you move forward, you will find doorways of opportunity beginning to open. As they do, continue to step through them, always remembering to submit your will each day to your heavenly Father. Eventually, you might find yourself as a full-time missionary or professional in Japan. Of course, you might find yourself in Alaska, if that is where God wants you.

How did God guide you? By giving you a principle to follow—that of taking the talents you currently possess and improving them for the Master. Since you are in the habit of submitting your will to Him each day and studying His Word, you should not continually worry, questioning if you are following God's will. He is certainly capable of, and willing to, step in and intervene at any time should it be necessary. As long as you are willing to follow, you can move ahead and rest well at night in the confidence of His leading.

Q. What suggestions do you have for educational preparation?
A. First let me say that in today's world an organization needs to have as few administrative layers as possible in order to be able to react with flexibility and quickly to opportunities. That principle doesn't just apply to business, it applies to God's work as well.

I suggest that you identify your natural interests and abilities and seek an education within those areas that you naturally enjoy and have abilities in. Visit with somebody in your intended field of service and get some advice from them.

Another area I would really like to underscore, to be a missionary, is that you have to be able to do quite a few different things. So instead of being a specialist in one area I would suggest that you diversify your training and seek a combination of skills that would meet the diverse needs of the work. Being a jack-of-all-trades works well on the front lines. Specializing is good for a university job, for a scientist who might require a Ph.D. for some area of service that needs a specialty. However, for general front-line work, having training in diverse fields of study is more important.

The local culture and language are absolutely vital to be able to communicate with the people you are trying to reach. Once you have identified the country that you are going to work in, God has opened the doors, and you are convinced that's where you're going to go, adopt that country as though it were your own. Train your mind to think and speak as if you were a local, try to adopt the accent. Even though you might be a North American or you might be from another country, when you adopt a country you should speak of it as being your own. For example, when I'm in Guyana I say, "We Guyanese are proud of our beautiful country." I do that on purpose. I am not Guyanese, but I've adopted that country and I speak of it as my own when I am there. And remember it is an honor when you are considered one of their own, when people say, "You are one of our own." That immediately gives you a status to reach people and build your influence.

Specifically in the area of aviation, pilots need to hold at least a commercial pilot's license and an instrument rating with a minimum of 500 hours experience. Twelve hundred hours is recommended especially for instrument flying, but 500 hours is the minimum. Aviation maintenance training is very important. Most pilots will have to do their own maintenance. Not every country requires it, and, in fact, in Guyana we are required to have someone else do our maintenance. But being a mechanic allows you to take better care of your aircraft.

Pilots are not just taxi drivers. In my opinion they are missionaries first. The airplane is just a way for them to get around. They should also consider training in health care as a registered nurse, licensed practical nurse, or maybe emergency medical technician. And education in counseling, industrial arts, evangelism—all of those are important for pilots. Because once they get to the place they are flying to, they immediately have to deal with the issues there.

Q. How do you choose a mission field to serve in?

A. There's a little bit of variety in the way that you could select a mission field. For some people like Paul, for example—God specifically called him to Macedonia. He wasn't thinking of going there before. So some people receive a specific calling to a specific area. For the majority, however, that is not the case.

I believe God plants an interest. Some people just dream of China, and they want to go to China. They love the language, and it just builds a passion for China. Others want to go to South America, others Africa. Whatever the desire and passion that develops in you, I believe it is from the Lord. And so that would be the very first area to look at when choosing a mission field—what area of interest do you have? Identify a continent, region, or country where your interests lie. Familiarize yourself with the country's history, geography, culture, and language. Go with a Maranatha trip or whatever, to the area that you would like to go. Develop contacts with the local church leadership because you will be working underneath their umbrella. Serving as a volunteer for a year is a nice, powerful way to get to know and develop contacts. If you know your church administration, your pastors, church and community leaders, as well as the members, it gives you the basis for being able to make that decision. Being responsible and dependable and a valuable contribution to the local work can almost assure that there will be a place for you to work there.

Q. How do you choose a means of support?

A. There is no one right way to meet your financial needs while working as a missionary. Some personality types feel more comfortable in a situation where all financial variables have already been defined. There are those who are very flexible and willing to launch with only minimal or no guarantee of funding. Most people fit in somewhere in the middle.

God is willing to work with all types of plans. Be aware, however, that He usually places a person outside of their comfort zone so that they will learn to trust Him with the unknowns. Mission service is always filled with a great number of surprises that must be placed in God's hands as one moves forward. And of course, don't forget that someday soon, every one of God's people will be forced into a position where all human support will be cut off. Following are several methods used by missionaries to cover personal needs while working overseas.

Denominational employment. Some persons have professions and skills that match the needs of a budgeted position overseas. These salaried positions are coordinated through the General Conference and Division Secretariat offices. The few positions that exist are usually for professional specialists.

Self-supporting organizations. These sponsoring organizations may have a fixed stipend or salary available for the missionary candidate. Some ask the candidate to raise their own support before they actually launch. These types of organizations generally have needs that range from general church planting to technical and professional needs.

Self-supporting individuals. Some prospective missionaries may have access to personal funds sufficient to cover their needs while working overseas. Others may depend on their skills to obtain a job and pay their way while working overseas (such as the apostle Paul did when he was making tents to support himself). Sources of funds may come from family members, friends, or other church members to cover a fixed amount each month. Frequently, a congregation may sponsor an individual as a full-time missionary or volunteer.

Divine support. This radical but thrilling method is about total trust in God to provide for our needs. It is what this book is all about—God's ability and willingness to provide for *all* of our needs while we concentrate on working for Him. This biblical method is to be found in Mark 6:7-13 and Luke 10:1-11, where Jesus sent His disciples out two by two with nothing in hand. They simply had to go out, trusting in God to provide for their needs. When they returned, Jesus asked them, in Luke 22:35, if they had lacked anything, and they joyfully answered, "Nothing."

Men such as George Mueller and Hudson Taylor are famous today because of their trust in God's ability to provide. Through sacrifice they moved forward confidently, and God did *exactly* as He had promised. He provided for all their needs according to His riches in glory. "The one who calls you is faithful and he will do it" (1Thessalonians 5:24, NIV).

A most fascinating reality is that all of God's children, regardless of what financial plan they choose, will one day be forced to adopt the plan of divine support, when all human aid will be cut off. I have no doubt that for most, this will be a most severe trial, and many will not pass the test.

Those who choose now to live under this beautiful principle will see God's hand revealed in their behalf. They will face future events with confidence and will be a tremendous encouragement to others who are forced into learning such trust for the first time.

If you feel called into mission service, I hope that this book will encourage you to experience the principle of divine support for yourself while it is still a choice. You will find that "the Lord's hand is not short-ened, that it cannot save; nor His ear heavy, that it cannot hear" (Isaiah 59:1, NKJV).

Q. Do you have advice for dealing with local church leaders and government officials?

A. First, acknowledge the responsibility of local church leaders to manage and safeguard church work in their territory. Coordinate your plans as much as possible with them and be flexible. Develop close working relationships with your mission or conference and union administration. Make a personal visit to administrators to determine how best you can help fulfill *their* mission. Become a face, not just a name. And recognize that differences in culture and vision can pro-duce frustration to both missionaries and local administration. It's also important to identify spiritually mature lay nationals who are willing to provide counsel.

A word of caution, though. There may be leaders who will try to micromanage everything in their field, including what God has called you to do, in spite of Ellen White counsels and denominational Work-ing Policy to the contrary. This management style will bring stress. At such times, constantly lay your case before the Lord and seek the counsel from those you trust.

A most important and critical area of management involves finances.

You have a responsibility to keep your donors informed. Financial information regarding your project should be reserved for those who have financial input. Resist pressure to provide confidential income sources and financial information to nondonors. However, permitting an occasional audit by the union or division is appropriate and will maintain confidence.

Concerning governments, while some countries may welcome missionaries with open arms, others perceive them with suspicion and hostility. Learn as much as you can from nationals and other missionaries about their attitudes and values. Always treat government officials with utmost respect. As a general principle, provide officials with only the information they request without volunteering more than needed. This includes even your own government embassy or consulate. And as much as is within your power, and in harmony with God's will, obey all laws and requirements.

It's important to remain completely clear of political movements or parties. Don't even express an opinion one way or the other. For us as foreigners and missionaries with a mission, politics is none of our business.

Q. What about staying in touch with family and supporters back home?

A. If you have a church family or group back home that is praying and perhaps providing financial support for you, keep them informed of your challenges and progress. Be honest about your difficulties and discouragements, but do not focus on the negative. Be optimistic. If you mention problems, focus on God's power to resolve them through prayer. If He already has solved the difficulty, make it a praise report.

Remember that what you write may return to the mission field, so carefully consider what you say and what attitude you convey in your report. Your influence back home may be greater than that in the mission field. When God intervenes on your behalf, let people see God at work.

Take advantage of technology as much as possible. Computers and email will facilitate communication. Digital cameras can be used to email pictures back to your donors and local church leaders. And don't forget to send out Thank-you notes to donors. Local supporters and volunteers also need to hear a word of gratefulness from you.

Finally, accept as many speaking appointments as possible. As you inspire and share God's blessing with others, you will be blessed in return.

Q. How do you measure success in God's work?

A. God has called people to be partners with Him in carrying out His work on earth. We should place our personalities, cultures, languages, skills, talents, and resources in His hands, to be used under His direction. The success of the work does not rest solely upon God, but depends to a great extent on our choices. Listen to this quote from *Prophets and Kings,* p. 263: "When God opens the way for the accomplishment of a certain work and gives assurance of success, the chosen instrumentality must do all in his power to bring about the promised result. In proportion to the enthusiasm and perseverance with which the work is carried forward will be the success given. God can work miracles for His people only as they act their part with untiring energy."

God generally does not overrule when there is bad management, misuse of funds, lack of vision, selfishness, carelessness, laziness, unwillingness to sacrifice, overcontrolling and unloving attitudes. Many projects fail, not because God ordained it, but because of our own errors and inflexibility. How great therefore is our responsibility to confess our weaknesses and implicitly follow His instructions. Here's another quote, this one from *The Desire of Ages,* p. 369: "If we plan according to our ideas, the Lord will leave us to our own mistakes."

There are many standards to measure success. However, in God's work it is not our responsibility to determine success. Our responsibility is to be found faithful to God's calling, to reflect His love to a dying world and prepare them for His coming. Nothing else counts! Not institutions, buildings, aircrafts, equipment, assets, wealth, influence, schools, or churches. Though the world normally uses these standards to measure its definition of success, we must realize that they are simply assets used to accomplish the mission.

As we meet together to lay down plans for God's work, it should be our constant objective to follow what Jesus did and taught. "Christ's method alone will give true success in reaching the people" (*The Ministry of Healing,* p.143). The gospel of Matthew includes the following: Preaching the message; healing the sick; raising the dead; driving out evil spirits; feeding the hungry; giving water to the thirsty; caring for the stranger; clothing the naked; visiting the sick and those in prison; making disciples of all nations and baptizing them; teaching them to observe all that Christ commanded (see Matthew 10:6-8; 25:35, 36; 28:19-20).

God has given the Seventh-day Adventist Church a very special message for this end time. It is a message for everyone, but in a special way it is for God's children, those who already know Him but do not understand what is at stake. As the enemy focuses on attacking God's character of love and justice, as revealed in Jesus, we are called to reveal in our lives the truth about God, His law, His character, and how to prepare for Jesus' soon return.

Q. What final thoughts do you have on being a missionary?

A. One's ministry overseas may not be as large as one's ministry back home. At home there are those who desperately need to hear that God is still alive and able and willing to provide for His children. Telling others of what God has done for *you* is one of your most important responsibilities.

Being a faithful steward is absolutely necessary to the continuance of God's blessings. Having a faith ministry is no excuse for bad money management.

When a church congregation decides to become directly involved in sponsoring an overseas missionary or project, it usually results in increased giving at the home church. A mission-driven church is a growing church. A wise church pastor will encourage his congregations to adopt mission projects.

Move through conviction of God's calling, not mere adventure seeking.

Believe God's promises literally and act accordingly. And always remember that God will "supply all your need according to His riches in glory" (Philippians 4:19, NKJV). "Our heavenly Father has a thousand ways to provide for us, of which we know nothing" (*The Desire of Ages,* p. 330).

Develop a willingness to take risks by moving forward in the face of unknown variables, and this could include a lack of resources. It is acceptable to feel terrified when advancing without sufficient funds. However, on such occasions, fall on your knees and lay God's promises out before Him, claiming each one. When His peace fills you, then make your move.

Remember the project doesn't have to last forever to be successful. Some projects pass through a window of opportunity for a short time only before it becomes impossible to continue. Closure of a project is not necessarily failure. Don't be afraid of failure. Rather, be afraid of not trying.

Play the game with the deck of cards that is dealt to you. If you wait for conditions to be ideal, you may never act. Move forward in obedience to God, regardless of how difficult the situation may seem. Remind yourself that the disciples were asked to feed the multitude with only five loaves and two fishes. They could have argued that obedience was impossible, as the resources looked insufficient to carry forward the task. By obeying they demonstrated that "we are to impart of that which we have; and as we give, Christ will see that our lack is supplied" (*Testimonies for the Church,* vol. 6, p. 345).

People are more important than things. The most valuable asset of an organization is its people. Take care of your people, and they will take care of the things.

God still asks us today, "What is that in thine hand?" (Exodus 4:2, KJV) Use it!

If you enjoyed this book, you'll enjoy these as well:

Chosen

Ron and Nancy Rockey. The true story of Ron Rockey's journey from prison to literal and spiritual freedom proves that God is behind and at work in all the storms in our lives to bring about a good end. Includes a personal study guide/self-help section.
0-8163-1900-6. Paperback.
US$12.99, Can$20.49.

In His Hands

Sophie Berecz and Arpad Soo. The exciting true story of God's miraculous protection of a Romanian Adventist pastor who smuggled literature behind the iron curtain. Imprisonment, divorce, poverty and ultimately, financial blessings all play a part in this amazing story.
0-8163-1903-0. Paperback.
US$12.99, Can$20.49.

Beyond the Veil of Darkness

Esmie Branner. A heart-pounding account of the struggles, hardships, and courageous triumph of a young Christian woman who refused to deny her faith in Christ despite the physical and mental abuse of a Muslim husband.
0-8163-1713-5. Paperback.
US$9.99, Cdn$15.49.

Order from your ABC by calling **1-800-765-6955**, or get online and shop our virtual store at **www.adventistbookcenter.com**.
  • Read a chapter from your favorite book
  • Order online
  • Sign up for email notices on new products

Prices subject to change without notice.